MAKING SPACE FOR GOD: AN INVITATION

by

Nicolas Stebbing CR &
Philippa Edwards OSB

Mirfield Publications

Published 2019 by Mirfield Publications
Community of the Resurrection
Stocks Bank Road
Mirfield, West Yorkshire
WF14 0BN

www.mirfield.org.uk

Cover by Michael Boag for Mirfield Publications.
Edited & typeset by Bruce Carlin for Mirfield Publications.

British Library Cataloguing in Publication Data. A catalogue record for this book is available from the British Library.

ISBN 978-0-902834-48-4

Making Space for God: An Invitation

Invitation into Space

Monastic life is a strange strange animal in this twenty first century. It may seem exotic, or irrelevant, a hangover from a distant past. What can it say to people today, caught up in the stress of daily life? We believe it has a lot to say that our world needs to hear. It offers us first a space. Life today is cluttered with things, people, stuff, noise, images and distractions. We lose a sense of who we are. Monasticism offers a space where we can find ourselves.

Benedictine monasticism has survived over 1500 years because Saint Benedict wrote a Rule which is full of quiet wisdom, balance and practical advice. It is a rule which is valued by monks and nuns, but also by large numbers of other Christians. Even many who have no Christian faith at all have found this Rule, this way of life, speaks good sense to them.

This book is not so much about the Rule as about the life which it helps some of us to live. We invite you simply to enter the space which this offers, to read our description of the life we live and love and to ask yourself how this could bring little changes to your life that will give it more meaning and help you to make more sense of what you are doing.

What we have written came out of many hours of fascinating conversations between the two of us, one Roman Catholic, one Anglican. Most of the actual writing was done by Fr Nicolas with direct contributions by Sr Philippa clearly indicated. It is a joint work, however, and we are glad to offer it as a witness to the deep unity of our Christian lives which lies beneath the apparent divisions of our churches.

1. Monasticism: a brief introduction

Monastic life is not peculiar to Christianity. Hindus and Buddhists had monks and nuns centuries before Christ. Even amongst the Jews, some communities existed around the time of Jesus which appear to have been monastic in character. John the Baptist may have belonged to one of these.

Christian monasticism began in the first centuries of the Christian era when individuals went out into the wide deserts of North Africa and the Middle East to fast and pray and to seek God in solitude. The most famous of these was St Antony of Egypt who is reckoned to be the father of the desert hermits. Often such men were alone; sometimes they lived together in loose communities. St Pachomius was one of the first to form a proper monastery in Egypt. St Basil was credited with being the real founder of monastic life in the Greek-speaking East. St Benedict was not the founder of monastic life in the West, but he wrote a Rule which gradually became accepted as the guiding rule of most monasteries in Western Europe during the Middle Ages.

Benedict was born in 480 AD in Italy and died around 547 AD. He was sent to study in Rome but was shocked by the decadent lifestyles of his fellow students and so left when he was eighteen and began monastic life in a cave in Subiaco. Scores of monks gathered round him there wanting to learn from him. It seems he was too strict and some of them actually tried to poison him! So then he moved to Monte Cassino where he established a more humane, well balanced way of monastic life. His famous Rule[1] is quite short and concentrates on the relations between

[1] There are many good translations of this Rule. The most commonly used now is RB1980, Editor Timothy Fry. The Liturgical Press, Minnesota 1982.

the brothers or sisters though it begins and ends with the final motive of monastic life: to serve God joyfully.

Italy in these years was overtaken by foreign invasions and constant violence. The Roman Empire in the West was collapsing. The Emperor in Constantinople tried to assert his authority over invading people from the north. Probably many who came to be monks at Monte Cassino were fleeing such violence. Benedict's monastery became a haven of peace in a sea of chaos. Finally, after Benedict's death the Lombards sacked the monastery. The monks fled to Rome with their Rule. A disaster at the time became an important step forward in the history of Europe. The monks became known to Pope Gregory the Great and it was he who began to push the story of Benedict and his Rule as the answer to the chaos of the age. Gradually the Rule became the inspiration of most of the monastic communities in Europe.

Monks and Religious

A monastery is a settled community of men or women living under vows. St Benedict says that monks (or nuns) 'live in monasteries and serve under a rule and an Abbot (or Abbess).'[2] That phrase sums up the three important factors: it is a community life; it is life under a rule, and it is life in obedience to the leader of the community. Members live a life of obedience structured around shared daily prayers (known as 'the offices'), a degree of silence and the common life. Some may live 'strictly enclosed' lives, hardly ever leaving the monastery. Others may travel a good deal but still feel themselves rooted in one monastic place. Some may teach or even run parishes. Others work at agriculture, home

[2] Rule of St Benedict (from now on cited as RB) 1:2

industries or computers to make a living. Quite often writing and art flourish in monasteries when there is the time and talent for it.

In the late Middle Ages, new orders grew up, of which the Franciscans and Dominicans are the best known. The men's branches of these orders were not monastic as they lived often on the road or in small houses in towns. They are often referred to as mendicant ('wandering') friars and their houses may be called convents. The women's branches of these orders were strictly enclosed like their Benedictine sisters and supported the friars by their prayers. Later, however, orders of sisters were founded in the Franciscan and Dominican traditions who were not enclosed but did practical 'works of mercy' – teaching, nursing, caring for orphans. This became the commonest form of women's religious life.

In the sixteenth century, a revolution took place with the founding of the Jesuits, who were free to say the offices privately and were not bound by tight rules of common life. Everything about their life was directed towards the work they did. They, and the various orders of men and women who followed in their tradition, are generally called 'apostolic religious'.

The term 'religious' covers all these different groups of men and women.

Anglicans and St Benedict

Henry VIII was famous for his wives, for his break with Rome, and for his destruction of monastic life. All the Protestant Reformers dispensed with monastic life on various theological or moral grounds. Henry's destruction was neither theological nor moral. He saw that the monasteries and religious orders were where the strongest opposition to his rejection of the Pope would be found. He also needed the money he could raise by selling off the monastic property, and he could gain support from the lay nobility by selling them those estates[3]. He used Thomas Cromwell as his agent in this and within a few years nothing was left of a flourishing monastic life.

Three centuries elapsed before religious life returned to the Church of England. Even now most Anglicans probably do not know there is such a thing as Anglican religious life. However, in the nineteenth century there was a revival of Catholic life in the Church of England, commonly referred to as the Oxford Movement which later grew into the Anglo-Catholic movement. They rediscovered the full sacramental life, a strong theology of the Church and a tradition of prayer that went back through the ages. This made them want the religious life, too.

The first Anglican communities were of sisters and began in the 1840's. They needed to prove to the church that they were not parasites or idle romantics and so they took on parish work, teaching, nursing and social care. At the same time they tended to have a monastic style of life, wearing traditional habits, saying a full office and committing themselves to prayer. They largely imitated their Roman Catholic sisters. By the end of the nineteenth century there were thousands of these Anglican sisters.

---

[3] An interesting parallel can be found in Zimbabwe from 2000 onwards. Robert Mugabe needed to break the power of the opposition and buy support from his followers. So he sent in his 'war vets' and others to take over white farmers' land without compensation. The farms, which were supposed to be given to the poor were mostly given to his own supporters, with disastrous consequences for the country. Similar stories can be told of life in Eastern Europe under Communism or indeed in the Roman Empire under Pompey and Caesar!

On the men's side, religious life began again with the Society of St John the Evangelist in 1865. In the 1890's both the Community of the Resurrection and the Society of the Sacred Mission came into existence. All these communities of men were largely priestly, did much in the way of missions and retreats and began mission work in South Africa and India. In the twentieth century various small Franciscan communities came together to form the Society of St Francis. Also in the twentieth century, after some abortive attempts, the first Benedictine community, Nashdom Abbey, was founded.

As with the Roman Catholic orders, the years since Vatican II (1962 onwards) have seen a steady decline in numbers as men and women have struggled to adapt the religious life to a changing world. Many communities have gone out of existence. It is hard to know what the future of religious life in the West will be.

When the ecumenical movement brought down the walls between Anglicans and Catholics, Catholic religious began to visit Anglican communities and said "You are all Benedictine monks (or nuns)", except of course the Anglican Franciscans. "No, we are not" we said. "Yes, you are." And they were right. It seems that Benedictine life was inherent in the Anglican Church and so religious life naturally took that form. Where did it come from?

First, when Archbishop Cranmer reduced the Roman Office to the Anglican version of Morning and Evening Prayer and made that compulsory for all priests, he created an Anglican devotional life that was centred on the same psalmody and scriptural reading that had formed monastic prayer. Though much attenuated, the structure and regularity of the daily office was the same.

Secondly, uniquely in England, most of the cathedrals in medieval times had been Benedictine monasteries. When the monastic life was destroyed, the cathedrals had their deans and chapters of canons who functioned much like a monastic chapter. They had their choirs which sang the daily office. The life of worship went on and was well attended by the laity. The liturgical praise of God came to be one of the cherished glories of the Church of England.

Thirdly, the two universities of Cambridge and Oxford had been largely religious foundations. After the monks had been banished, the fellows and dons remained largely clerical and unmarried. They and their students lived a common life, ate together, prayed together at compulsory chapel worship, and continued the Benedictine practice of sober, sound learning. One must not claim too much: there were many abuses, much laxity and many failures. Yet the principle remained, and when the founders of Anglican religious life in the nineteenth century looked around for a model, they naturally replicated the life of their Colleges. Common life, common prayer and sound learning could be seen as a basis of Benedictine monasticism.

All this happened so naturally it was largely unnoticed. It was only as Roman Catholic Benedictine life came to renew itself in the twentieth century, and as ecumenical contacts drew the two sides together that we realised how naturally Benedict finds himself in the Anglican Communion. He was always there!

2. Why Join a Monastery?

Nicolas' Story

I was born in Harare and have always loved Zimbabwe. I have never wanted to live anywhere else. My mother was born in the country. My father came there when he was 19. Mum was a very keen hockey player and coached hockey, swimming and diving. She was also very politically aware and we grew up largely in opposition to the right wing politics of Ian Smith's Government.

During our early years we were sent to Sunday School, first at the local Anglican church which we disliked as the Vicar was boring. (I later discovered he was a very good priest who did great work, but had no talent with small children). Then we went to a Full Gospel Sunday School where we enjoyed singing evangelical choruses. In due course a new Anglican church opened near us, with a young priest who was very good with teenagers and we started going there. Going to church was not an unusual thing to do in those days. Our youth club was based at the church so we met our friends there. Very soon I became fascinated by church. I asked to become a server, and used to feel that I was almost in heaven when I was serving at the altar. By the time I was 13, I had decided that I wanted to be a priest. Our family experience of church was very mixed. My father came to church three times a year as he reckoned he had had too much of it when he was young. Mum was as regular and as keen as I was. My sisters later in life became good attenders, and my brother dropped away almost completely. Why did I become such a fanatic? That is a mystery.

Being keen on Church didn't make me any better than my friends. I wasn't spectacularly wicked (none of us was then) but nor was I very good. I was certainly lazier than most boys, and so got beaten more often at school. That gave me a certain reputation for naughtiness which I quite enjoyed! I regret the laziness now. The two things I would really like to have learned well at school, Latin and French, still have shaky foundations. Interestingly, we had no religious education at all. We got that at home or in church, not in school.

As school came to an end, my own religious enthusiasm moved from just enjoying the worship to actually caring about sacraments. When I was 18, I returned to confession after a lapse of three years. The priest told me to visit St Augustine's Mission, Penhalonga. I had never heard of it, but wrote to them, and within days had arranged a visit. A friend and I drove down in his mother's car. I was stunned by the place. The mission is in a beautiful setting, on a hill with higher hills all around. The buildings were simple but attractive. Ten Fathers of the Community of the Resurrection lived there in what seemed to me astonishing holiness. So did some white sisters from England and some black local sisters. Most of the brethren said their own Mass each day. Seven times a day they gathered to recite the offices. Silence rules pertained in the house for quite a lot of the day. I had the library to myself and lovely countryside outside. Meanwhile the Fathers taught in school, or ran large mission districts to north and south. I thought I was in heaven. I was reading as much as I could about Anglo-Catholic history and saw this as the summit of it all – very Catholic religion along with a heroic ministry to the poor.

I didn't know then that all this was soon to go: the reforms of Vatican II affected Anglicans as well as Roman Catholics. I didn't know either that this priory was probably the unhappiest priory in the Community. Brethren got sent there because they couldn't get on with others. They immersed themselves in work or disappeared into the rural areas to visit churches and schools. Their legacy to the Church was great but it never gave birth to a local African form of religious life. In a way they were not interested in that. They were missionaries from England doing a job. So someone like me who wanted to join the Community, but was not from England, was an anomaly.

The Community of the Resurrection was founded in 1892, in Oxford by a group of priests led by Charles Gore. It was intended to be a community of priests serving the church in whatever ways it could. It quickly settled into a pattern of parish missions, preaching, academic work and training men for the priesthood. In 1898, as all the brethren were committed Christian Socialists, it moved to Mirfield in Yorkshire, in order to be amongst the industrial working class. In 1902, the Community was invited to South Africa to help the Church there recover from the Boer War. That began a century of work largely in the Johannesburg area. In 1914 they sent two brothers to take over the mission at St Augustine's, Penhalonga.

The brethren had a huge impact on me. I began to pray much more seriously. I now had a dream, to become a CR Father as well as a priest. I wanted to work among Africans. CR helped open my eyes further to the injustice suffered by African people in this country ruled by whites. When I started at university a few weeks later I found myself living in a hostel with black and coloured students. It takes a long time to overcome a racist upbringing, if one ever does, but CR started me off on a journey, both spiritual and political, which I have been on ever since.

I loved university. I loved the Latin and Greek I was doing, but I had still not learned to work properly so I failed my first year. After a brief and unhappy time working in a bank, I came back on a shoe string and finally managed an undistinguished arts degree. I made lots of friends, went to some really great parties, did in the end learn quite a bit about the Bible and a certain amount of Greek. Every vacation saw me back at Penhalonga for at least a week, hitchhiking the 160 miles each way, which introduced me to the joys of hitchhiking; I kept that up for decades after. I also went to the Community's house in Johannesburg. In South Africa, the Community's work was very urban. Its ministry had been in Sophiatown and Orlando for over 40 years. Trevor Huddleston, already famous as a campaigner against apartheid, was a member of the Community and had written *Naught for Your Comfort* in the house I was visiting. We were constantly aware of the vicious South African form of apartheid, far worse than Rhodesia's, and it was exciting to be part of the small group of people who crossed the racial lines and, in whatever way they could, opposed the racism of the country.

In 1967, I made my first trip to England. It was amazing: Flower Power, Carnaby St, London and the English winter with my first ever sight of snow. I also got to Mirfield, the Mother House of our Community and asked the Superior if I could join the Community right away. Definitely not, he said. And he was right. I was too young, too immature and needed a wider experience of life. I went off, finished my degree and then went and taught Latin at St David's, Bonda, a mission school for

African girls, run by Sisters from Whitby[4]. It was a wonderful year. It was my first real contact with Africans and it was life changing. At the same time, living with nuns confirmed my own desire for religious life. A year later I moved to St Anne's, Goto, a newer school in the Wedza district. It was hotter and more basic there. The school was not as good as Bonda, but I had probably the happiest three years of my life. I learned Shona (the local language). I came to understand far more of the political attitudes of black people. I effectively changed sides. We had wonderful evenings drinking beer and talking politics, and I learned quite a lot about Shona culture as well. When the time came for me to go to Mirfield to train for the priesthood I left in tears.

I was supposed to spend two years at the College at Mirfield, and then return to Rhodesia to work for the Church. I was impatient. As soon as I got to Mirfield I went to the Superior and asked to join CR without bothering to become a priest. He sent me packing again, and he was right, again. I had eighteen months at the College, enjoyed it, hated it, longed for Africa, made lots of friends, some of whom I still have; but as soon as I could, I was back in Rhodesia with the civil war steadily escalating. I was to be curate in a plush, largely white suburb in Salisbury. That was great fun with an excellent parish priest and wonderful friends. But living with well off whites was not good for me; I enjoyed the affluent life style but was insensitively critical of their racial attitudes. It didn't help that the civil war was now raging, and naturally polarised attitudes. I wanted, anyway, to be in a rural area working with Shona people. The Bishop moved me to St John's, Chikwaka, a mission with a children's home and seven out stations. It

[4] The Anglican Order of the Holy Paraclete

was wonderful! I went round on a motor bike, learned more Shona, enjoyed the bush and found the increasing war both frightening and exciting. But then one evening four Dominican sisters and three Jesuits were shot dead at the next door mission. That was devastating. I thought God would look after people like us. Evidently not. I've spent the rest of my life struggling with that knowledge. God is good. God loves us, but it doesn't mean he protects us from all evil. Evil is shot through our life, even the most Christian life. The agony of the Cross and Christ's suffering for our sin is never far away. Six months later, the African sisters on my mission said it was time for me to go, otherwise "something terrible will happen." As it happened I had already asked to join the Community of the Resurrection and been accepted. After 10 years of waiting I could finally go. I could never say in the future that I had entered in too much of a rush!

Looking back after nearly forty years, it is hard to remember much about the noviciate. The Community was in a state of shock as the Superior had left in scandalous circumstances. There were four of us in the noviciate and of course we squabbled a lot. We didn't have much teaching or formation. It was expected formation would just happen, and maybe it did. Three of us were already priests. My big problem emerged early and has remained ever since: I am as sure as I can be that God wants me in CR. In that sense I never 'tested' my vocation to religious life as one is supposed to do. I assumed it. I was also sure that I wanted to be in Zimbabwe and was pretty sure God agreed with me. That of course was more doubtful. Anyway, after two years of making a fuss, I persuaded the Community to let me and the South African novice go to Johannesburg to complete our noviciate there. This, we hoped, would start an African noviciate which would help form an African style CR that wouldn't be governed all the time by English assumptions. That never happened, but that's another story.

Johannesburg was exciting. Politics were our daily bread. We broke the law every day by having black people to stay with us, or by going to Soweto without permits. Wonderful South African opposition leaders like Desmond Tutu, Helen Joseph and Beyers Naude came to see us; or, if they were under house arrest, we went to see them. We attended court cases where priests and bishops were convicted of riotous assembly, or, once, a treason trial including one of our priests. Life was very different from Mirfield. We had cars; we could go out to see people. We made friends with the Little Sisters of Jesus[5] in Soweto. We met Jesuits and Dominicans. We went to political meetings and enjoyed being watched by the police. And I tried, in my usual arrogant way to reform the Community from the bottom end. Naturally, this created tensions. Brethren put up with it for a while but simply went on with their own lives. Work came first, and the work was good. Community life happened in that we lived together, ate together and prayed together but no one wished to think about what form this life should take in the future. Brethren were really not interested in that.

I did quite a bit of study in those years, discovering to my surprise that I was quite good at it, whereas in the past I had been pretty bad. Ten years had given me some maturity and experience so I did well at Missiology, and learned some Zulu and some Afrikaans. After four years I went back to England and did a three month course with the Jesuits, including

---

[5] A wonderful Catholic order of contemplative sisters living amongst and working with the poor, inspired by Charles de Foucauld

the Spiritual Exercises. This was in preparation for my Final Vows. The question remained the same. I told God I wanted to be a member of CR for the rest of my life but I needed to know I would spend my life in Africa. God made it clear (silently of course) that I could not set conditions on what he asked. I knew that, of course, but that never stopped me trying. So I made my profession at Mirfield and returned to South Africa to continue as chaplain to a children's home, do some more studies in missiology, give retreats and try to pray. During all this time my beloved Rhodesia was changing to Zimbabwe. I visited frequently but had to agree with the majority in CR that the time had come for us to leave the great mission we were running. This seemed to me an opportunity to try and live a form of religious life that was not simply a foreign mission. We needed to be Zimbabwean, to be more committed to prayer, and have a different, less missionary profile. However, most brethren in the Community disagreed so the chance to start a new kind of CR in that country was lost.

We had the same problem in South Africa. We were passionately committed to the struggle against apartheid and could think of little else. Most of the Brethren were English and never really identified with South Africans. They were in conflict with most of the whites politically, and separated from the blacks culturally. They did not learn the languages. They did not want to think of new ways of living the CR life. I was not skilled at presenting my ideas in a non-conflictual way so my various attempts to change people's thinking got nowhere.

By 1987 I was in a state of depression brought on by work, frustration with CR and a love affair which was never going to work out. My fellow South African was in a similar state and the Superior decided it was time for us to come back to England to work things out. I came back for one year and have stayed for thirty! Why have I stayed despite my constant longing to be back in Africa?

First, I found that life in the more monastic atmosphere of our Mother House was richer than life in the Johannesburg priory and seemed to be where God wanted me to be. Religious life in the Western world is in crisis and needs refounding. There were good ideas and a sense of movement here that showed hope for the future. I wanted to be part of that. By contrast, the Community in South Africa was stuck in the past. They wanted simply to keep on with the kind of work they had done for decades. They had a very English perception of what was needed and did not listen to what South Africans or Zimbabweans were saying. Much as I enjoyed life in Johannesburg, it had no future.

Second, within the Community I found myself as infirmarian, caring for the elderly. To my surprise, I enjoyed it and felt it important that we should do this work ourselves. Many communities had handed over their sick and elderly brethren to outsiders to care for. This didn't seem right. We could not claim to be a Christian community unless we cared for each other. Caring for the elderly is hard work, but it is important to keep them within the family. Thousands of people throughout England have to look after elderly and disabled relations and so should we. Close contact with these older brothers also enriches us, passing on the traditions from the past and teaching us that other people come first, ahead of our own concerns. I needed to learn that! Among those I cared for were Trevor Huddleston who was very difficult and really wonderful. Through him I had amazing experiences visiting Delhi, meeting Nelson Mandela and many other great people in England. Religious life has its surprises!

I found myself doing more retreats around England, and spiritual direction at our College. More things were added as I took on an ecumenical work which involved frequent travel to Europe and that was really interesting. I remember remarking to a German sister as we arrived at a beautiful monastery in Switzerland, "Aren't we lucky to be able to come to places like this, and call it work?" Academic life also made its appearance; I began to visit Romania just after the Revolution in 1989 and became enchanted by the Romanian Orthodox who managed to come through the Communist years with parish churches and many monasteries still intact. I ended up doing research on Spiritual Fathers in Romania and came to love the country almost as much as Zimbabwe. Life has certainly been full over the past 30 years.

In 2003 a new Superior sent me to South Africa for nine months to see if I could discover a new way forward for CR. It was a wonderful and confusing experience, immersing myself in post-apartheid South Africa. The short answer to the question was that there was no future for CR. It was not clear what was required in that fascinating but changing society; it was clear that CR could not provide it. In 2006, the last few brethren returned to England. At the same time my involvement in Zimbabwe increased. Soon I found myself helping the church there; then in 2009 some of us started a charity, Tariro, to work with young people in need. At last, the two ends of my life came together: I need to be in England to raise money for the work in Zimbabwe, and I need to visit Zimbabwe regularly to see the money is well spent. I get monastic life and Zimbabwe. What could be better?

What have I learned through all this?

- Despite lots of difficulties, tensions, complaints and even tantrums, life in CR has been richly fulfilling;
- We don't always get what we want when we follow God and we may have to admit that what we wanted was not right! If we stay faithful to God, what we get turns out to be right. That is a bit simplistic, but largely true;
- I am still in the middle of the story. I want to know more about how monastic life under the Rule of St Benedict really works. I have lived it to some extent but I haven't really understood it. I am still trying to do that.

Philippa's Story

I was born into a Roman Catholic family in Pretoria, South Africa, on a Friday in Lent in 1946. My parents were very loving but I was a sickly, unhappy child, with a tendency to be a drama queen. Once when I was about two, as my parents drove off to a dinner party leaving me with the nanny, I wailed, "My heart is bleeding!" (the imagery derived from a picture of the Sacred Heart).

When I was nine my father, a barrister, very unhappy with the apartheid regime, decided to emigrate to what was then Rhodesia. We lived first in Bulawayo and later in what was then called Salisbury (now Harare) and for several years my sister and I were at boarding-school in Mutare. There I developed the habit of going to daily Mass although this was not compulsory; I found both the Scripture readings and the Eucharist sustained and strengthened me. But when the headmistress told me she had had a dream about my becoming a nun I decided that if messages from God were to be given through dreams they would have to be my own. I spent the next seven years in flight from the very thought of the religious life, though at that time most Catholic girls would at least give it fleeting consideration, and two of my mother's many sisters had joined different orders.

I read English at university in Salisbury. There I met Mike, now Fr Nicolas Stebbing. We both had small parts in a production of *The Carmelites* by Georges Bernanos. (I later found that these Carmelites had been imprisoned during the French Revolution with the Stanbrook community). I continued to go to daily Mass at the university chaplaincy. I recall being powerfully struck by the readings on the feast of St Mary Magdalen, from the Song of Songs, 'I sought him whom my soul loves,' and the Gospel passage describing the meeting of Mary Magdalen with the Risen Christ on Easter morning.

As soon as possible after graduation I left Rhodesia for 'Swinging London.' There I had a series of dead-end jobs on the edge of the publishing world. Then I was inspired (by seeing on television *The Corn is Green* by Emlyn Williams) to help to change the world by discerning and developing the potential of primary school children. This led to my doing a six-week course designed to turn graduates in any subject into infant teachers. I spent almost a year failing to teach infants in schools ever further east – Aldgate, Stepney, Poplar. Then I heard from a friend that a family in Rome needed a nanny to look after their two small children, and, as it was the end of term and feeling I had nothing to lose, I took the first train I could get.

As it happened almost all of the handful of contacts I had in Rome were priests or nuns. One of these told me of Mass in English on the first Friday of each month at the Irish Augustinian Seminary. There I had an experience which I later discovered echoed that of St Antony of Egypt, reckoned to be the father of monasticism. I heard the words of the Gospel, "Come, follow me" as directed to me personally. I said "Yes" without knowing what it implied. On the way back to the Italian family, I realised that I was feeling far from well. When two boys aged about 12 rushed at me with plastic batons – part of carnival fun as it was close to Shrove Tuesday – I burst into tears. It seems to me now that God had been trying to get through to me for years but it was only when all my human resources were at a low ebb – I was sickening for 'flu, broke, in a strange country – that he got through.

During Lent I sought guidance through the Bible and prayer, and by the beginning of the Easter Vigil I'd decided that the thought of becoming a nun was sheer masochism. However, by the end of the Vigil, I had made up my mind in the opposite direction. For a while I thought I should join a teaching order, mainly because I'd made such a mess of teaching. But I felt attracted to the contemplative life in a vague romantic way, having seen films both about my patron saint at baptism, St Thérèse of Lisieux, and St Bernadette. I had a notion that as a contemplative I could go straight as an arrow to God, leaving behind all clutter. Little did I know how much clutter can accumulate through simply staying in the same place long enough! I had a phase when I thought God must want me to join the strictest order I could find. Fortunately, a wise old nun told me, "God wants you to be happy!" I wrote to all the monastic addresses I could get hold of – including a Carmel in the United States, stating that

I couldn't sing, and asking to come and stay inside the enclosure, as a Cistercian monk had advised.

The most welcoming answer I received was from the abbess of Stanbrook. She invited me to come as an aspirant "as soon as possible" after my return to England. A friend was giving a party on the Saturday, so I decided to go in on the Monday, which was the day after Pentecost. It was beautiful May weather and every day seemed to be a feast day. The novice mistress, Sr Maria, struck me as being radiantly in love with God. Various signs connected with books seemed to indicate strongly that Stanbrook was the right community for me. For example, my father had given my sister *In This House of Brede* by Rumer Godden, a wholly uncharacteristic choice, and the cover with Stanbrook's pink-and-white striped tower, caught my eye the moment I entered the guest room when I visited my parents, who were then living in Gaborone, Botswana, for my farewell visit before entering the monastery.

I entered in October 1970 and received the Habit six months later, on Easter Monday. In the northern hemisphere the cycle of the seasons is a powerful symbol of the death and resurrection of Christ. I had experienced three springs of this sort before I entered Stanbrook, but the spring of my clothing was a revelation. My first monastic Lent was made even harder than it would otherwise have been by a postal strike which went on week after week, which meant I had no communication at all with my family. Contact with friends was of course completely out of the question. Then Easter came. In addition to the power of the liturgy I was amazed and thrilled by the different shades and textures of green visible from my cell window which looked onto a large pond overhung with willow trees. The day of my clothing was the first day the heating was turned off and I returned to my cell after the clothing ceremony to find the windows flung wide open and the cell full of the scent of daffodils.

During the four and a half years before I left the noviciate to join the community proper I had many companions. There were always at least five of us, and sometimes as many as nine. I made many friends for life. Many of my companions were extremely gifted people – one an artist, another a composer, and I knew I wasn't in their league at all. But Sr Maria told me that I had the gift of poverty of spirit and a great capacity for God, the biggest compliment I have ever been paid. Gradually I have come to recognise that these qualities make it much easier for me to share in the kenosis of Christ[6] – and therefore in his resurrection. One of my greatest joys was beginning to learn to pray. I had a strong desire to give myself completely to God. The humanity of St Benedict's Rule, the sense of humour and lightness of touch which seemed to me to characterise the English Benedictine Congregation, Sr Maria's inspirational teaching based on profound love and knowledge of Scripture, and the warmth of the welcome I received from the community all confirmed my sense that I had come home after a long exile.

I was on Cloud Nine for years after entering Stanbrook. I was filled with a deep peace, joy and a sense of wonder at the beauty all around me, in the liturgy, in nature and in people. I felt a strong pull to a life spent in the praise of God.

---

[6] His renunciation of the Divine nature in the Incarnation.

I made my temporary vows on Easter Sunday, and my final vows three years later on Easter Thursday. Sr Maria told me that my whole life would be marked in a special way by the death and resurrection of Christ. At my Solemn Profession I sang, “I am married to him whom angels serve; sun and moon marvel at his beauty”.

Then life began in earnest. I was given jobs in the infirmary and in the kitchen which seemed to me to fall very definitely into the category of ‘impossible tasks,’ as referred to in Chapter 62 of the Rule of St. Benedict. It is an astonishing chapter considering that it was written in the 6th century. The monk is told that after dialogue with the Abbot he must in faith obey. It is an example of how this life can help a person to grow, to discover or develop talents they had no idea they had. I found I had a ‘good bedside manner’ which helped me to make some wonderful connections with the remarkable old nuns who were in the infirmary at the time. I recall with special affection Dame Mary. Once, when I was putting her to bed she asked me how I was and I responded that I had had an abominable day, going from one victim of a tummy bug epidemic to another all day. She said, with her sweet smile, “Well, my dear, you’re the light of my eyes. Put that in your pocket and keep it there.”

The kitchen was another area which I found impossible to start with. The Abbess, Dame Elizabeth Sumner, had trolleys especially made for me the same height as the stove so that I could slide rather than lift the enormous pots necessary to feed a community of over sixty. Two of us were sent to the Worcester Polytechnic to do a cookery course and I remember feeling as we entered the kitchen for the evening practical session, 'Abandon all hope, ye who enter here.'[7] But I have come really to enjoy cooking and giving pleasure to the community through food, 'the love of God made edible.'

My inability to sing has been a severe trial, both to myself and others. Dame Felicitas took me under her wing before my solemn profession to help me to sing the profession antiphons. She assured me that on the eve of my profession I sang them all in tune – but on the day itself I did not! However for a time I was able to take regular turns at leading the Office.

A series of crises ensued. Two of my closest friends left. They tried to persuade me to leave also, asking me if I really wanted to spend my life rotting in the monastery. I said "Well, yes. 'Unless the grain of wheat falls into the ground and dies it remains only a single grain…'[8]" But I was unsettled.

A big event was the illness and death at 54 of Sr Rosaline, with whom I had worked in the kitchen. She had a wonderful sense of humour and a Scripture text for every occasion. On a July day as we toiled over a hot stove she quoted Habakkuk, 'He flags whose soul is not at rights with God!'[9] Though in great pain she was really alive until she died, singing, making jokes, with a word for each of us on her last evening. When the abbess told her that the bridegroom was coming she said "Not a moment too soon". Her last words were, "Amen Alleluia!"

At some point the feast day of my patron, the Welsh Jesuit martyr St. Philip Evans, was changed to the anniversary of his death, July 22nd, the feast of St. Mary Magdalen. The Gospel passage which narrates the

---

[7] Sign over the gate of Hell in *Inferno*, from *The Divine Comedy* by Dante Alighieri
[8] John 12:24
[9] Habakkuk 2:4

story of the meeting of Mary Magdalen with the risen Jesus on Easter morning is of course read on that day, as well as on the Tuesday of Easter Week, which has on occasion coincided with my birthday.

About this time, in connection with a meeting I was organising, I met a psychotherapist which led to six months' therapy with her. This was a most exciting time. I had a tremendous number of waking visions and significant dreams culminating in an experience of re-birth and resurrection on Christmas Day, a Sunday that year.

It had been suggested that I do some serious study and, eventually, as a means of discerning the way ahead I went to St Beuno's for a long retreat. It was decided that I should do an Ignatian course in spiritual direction at All Saints, Margaret Street. St. Ignatius structured his spiritual exercises on the life, death, and resurrection of Christ.

The patient listening and wisdom of my spiritual director, a married ex-Anglican priest, Paul King, provided great support. My own ministry of spiritual direction has given me enormous joy. I am very conscious what a privilege it is to listen to another human being speaking from the heart, and have discovered that to hear anybody's story is to love them.

For a long time the community had been discussing the possibility of moving from Worcestershire. Our numbers had gone down and the average age up, and the monastery was expensive to maintain and to heat. However, some of us were very unhappy about the move for various reasons. Eventually four of us were given a year's leave of absence. We spent the first two months at Douai Abbey near Reading and then were accommodated in an empty presbytery in the picturesque village of East Hendred. It soon became clear that I was incompatible with the other three, and the abbess suggested that I spend the rest of my year visiting other monasteries, in England, Ireland and the United States, with a view to possibly changing my stability. This was a very difficult time. I was a fish out of water. At the end of the year, with great relief I returned to Stanbrook.

The next big challenge was putting the huge Stanbrook library onto a data base, preparatory to packing all 37,000 volumes. Sr Maria, back from twenty years as a hermit, was librarian and I her assistant.

We moved, in May 2009, to Wass in North Yorkshire. Our new Monastery was built both to fit in with its environment, and also to be environmentally friendly in the ways it used and conserved energy. An added bonus was its proximity to Ampleforth, a male Benedictine Community, with which we might hope to have closer links.

It was nevertheless a great uprooting after 170 years of stability. The bereavement aspect was emphasised by the death of the cat within weeks of our arrival. Later that year Sr Clare and Sr Maria died within three weeks of each other. It was very hard to lose our beautiful church, our established garden and our network of friends, and in my case, my directees. But there were good surprises, among them the beauty of the landscape and the freedom to walk in the forest. During our first snowy winter, to my astonishment I found that I have a good eye for photography and have greatly enjoyed taking photographs, especially of landscapes and wild flowers. I have discovered that when one really looks, everything in nature is beautiful, even mud and slugs.

Our beautiful new Church, completed in 2015, has transformed our lives. From the start its atmosphere has been conducive to prayer and its excellent acoustic and organ enhance the liturgy. It could not be more different from he neo-Gothic Pugin church in Worcestershire, but is a worthy successor to it.

I have learnt a good deal through the turbulent years. My desire to give myself completely to God remains, but I have realised that the mode of the giving is not important. I have come to see that sharing in the self - emptying of Christ is one side of a coin of which the fullness of life is the other. I have understood that God looks after all the details of our lives in a most remarkable way and that his timing is perfect. I have experienced the truth of St Benedict's promise that our hearts will be enlarged and that we'll run with the unspeakable sweetness of love along the way of God's commandments[10]; and that love casts out fear.[11] Two images that come to me are of a surfer riding a huge wave, or a giant condor soaring through the air currents. Yet again death has been followed by resurrection.

---

[10] RB Prologue 49

[11] 1 John 4:18

3. Space: Openness to God

A guest coming for the first time into a monastery can find it very strange. With luck he or she will be warmly welcomed and taken to a room. The room is simply furnished. He is left alone. If he walks down the corridor to the chapel he may meet one or two monks or nuns; they may smile but probably won't greet him. Chapel when he reaches it is large and welcoming but silent. Brothers coming in don't talk to one another; they don't stop for conversations. They simply slip quietly into choir. After the service the guest may find herself in a brief conversation before the meal, which is then eaten in silence. Everyone else seems to know what to do, where to find the food, where to put one's plate.

This can be a bit alienating at first but most people do adapt surprisingly quickly. They realise what a relief it is not to have to greet everyone they meet, to stop and ask how they are. There may be thirty or forty people in the house but they don't impinge on your space. They have learned not to crash through life, closing doors quietly, not chatting in corridors. This silence is not negative. It is warm and welcoming. You are free to be yourself and to start looking for God.

Most monasteries inhabit large spaces. Even a moderately sized community needs a big building to live in and these tend to be set in large grounds. The space speaks to us of God. God is not small and big spaces help us to realise that God is not to be domesticated, though he is often very gentle and loving. In a monastery the space is where we meet God. A guest is not programmed into some particular way of meeting God. The monastery walls and the grounds create a space in which you are free to wander. You may find God in Chapel, in front of the Blessed

Sacrament; or you may find him while reading a book in your room, or maybe by the fish pond or on the open road.

It is also not just the grounds that provide the space; everything about the life is designed to do that. The first thing the guest may find in his room is the daily timetable. This is important: it means you can find meals and services without having to ask anyone. The timetable sets the structure for the day, and by establishing the points at which corporate things happen it creates space between those points.

Likewise, the sisters or brothers are concerned to produce meals and sing services in a way that does not create a fuss but provides that warm and friendly space where you can relax and feel well looked after. You don't have to try hard. You just sit and wait and God will come to you.

Quite often guests will tell us what a wonderful effect we have had on their lives. They have loved the silence; they have loved the devotion with which the brothers sing the psalms; they have been treated with courtesy and respect. Everyone has been so helpful in their discovering so many new things about God. This is humbling, and often surprising. We don't feel much of this is true. We sing, but we hear the wrong notes, the discordancies, the over dominating voices. We think the silence is badly kept and we certainly don't feel much peace since our life is so busy. Yet, this is the mystery and the proof of God's presence. What we do seems to make it possible for God to come into this place and act directly on our guests. It is God who is at work, not us. This is good for us as it assures us we are not wasting our time; God really is doing things here. At the same time, there is no cause for us to be proud or conceited about our brilliant counselling skills or our amazing music since it wasn't those things at all which our guests met. God's Holy

Spirit comes silently and gently into every place where there are people. In a monastery it is easier for God to meet people who have relaxed their guard and are open and generous to receive what comes. It is one of our joys to be able to watch this happening and give thanks for it.

The modern world and modern people are work-oriented. Work is good. It provides us with the means to live. It gives us fulfilment as we exercise our skills and talents. It brings us into contact with others. But if we get too focussed on our work we can ignore the most important reason for human existence, which is simply to be, to be here for God. The monastic life-style makes a statement about God. It says that God exists and that he is important. And simply because the monks and nuns are there, they create a space for God. Our world needs that space.

Creating a space takes work. You have to clear that space. Our world is cluttered. Our society is so affluent that even the poor have piles of possessions such as their parents or grandparents never dreamed of. We believe we need these things, but we don't. Getting rid of possessions, furniture, clothes, boxes of mementos can be very liberating. Putting aside one's phone, turning off the computer, not looking at Facebook for a whole day can seem scary at first, but then we learn to look again at other things, and people. An academic in America told me recently how he looked out of his window on a beautiful spring day and saw a host of students, every one of whom was looking at a phone screen. Do we see God's creation around us?

A space is not enough. What goes into that space? Jesus tells of a man who managed to clear an unclean spirit out of himself. The spirit comes back and 'finds the house swept clean and put in order. Then it goes and brings seven other spirits more evil than itself, and they go in and dwell there. And the final plight of that man is worse than the first.'[12] As we clear space around us we need to put things into it that symbolise something new. Or, we need to regard this newly created space as space kept for God. That is what monasteries are, and it may be one of the most important gifts they offer to a confused and crowded world. We create space, and we know what that space is for.

Music space

Music creates space and fills space. Music is a very important part of monastic life. It is also central to Christian life since it fills so much of the space given to worship. It will be useful to look more closely at this.

English cathedrals and most ancient parish churches have a space in front of the altar where two sets of pews face each other. This is where the choir sit. To people outside the Anglican tradition it may seem a strange place to put them, facing each each other. Many churches now have the choir behind the altar facing the congregation. Their job is clearly to perform, both to sing fine music and to lead the congregation in worship. Other churches have the choir at the back of the church encouraging the singing from behind. Why put them in front of the altar and facing each other?

They are there because that is how monks and nuns in the Western church have always sat when praying together in church. Traditionally they had to spend many hours singing the psalms. This is hard work so the task was split in two: each half of the choir sang alternate verses to each other. Not only did this make it easier to sing but it also made worship a kind of dialogue or conversation. That makes it much more

---

[12] Luke 11:24-26

interesting. It helps to build community life when people have to listen to each other as well as speak or sing to each other. Each side had to listen carefully for the ending of the other side's verse so that they could all come in on time. This kind of singing from side to side is known as 'antiphonal' singing.

Singing together is great fun. Rugby teams do it; pub drinkers do it; Christians do it in church and it helps to build up a sense of community and involvement in a common activity. There are problems though. If everyone wants to join in you must either have a very simple set of words and a catchy tune that can easily be imitated and sung. Or you need to have the words on paper or on a screen. That produces a particular kind of singing which can be very enjoyable and even inspiring, but can also become monotonous. It can also produce hymns with very little theological content. Traditional Anglican hymns have good solid tunes which last for decades and good theology through which, if truth be told, the average church goer gets his or her main Chrisitian education. Such hymns as *Immortal, invisible, God only wise* or Charles Wesley's *Love Divine all love's excelling* are good examples of this. They are quite hard to sing well especially if you sing all the musical parts available.

Monastic life has relied on Gregorian plainsong for most of its singing of psalms and hymns. This is always sung antiphonally, creating that sense of dialogue. In itself this is important to the formation of a monk or nun as it teaches (or should teach!) us to listen to each other. If a monastic choir sings well together it probably means the community is getting on well with each other. If the singing falls apart and different voices dominate it is quite likely that there are conflicts in the community. Gregorian plainsong (simply called The Chant) has become quite popular in recent years and can be found on many CDs. Many people find it simply restful to listen to, whether sung in Latin or in English. It creates the space which our monastic churches offer. It speaks to believers of a God who is infinite and yet open and accepting; those who don't believe in God still find it opens up a space for them to think and feel differently from other kinds of music.

The Chant is a complex form of music with rules we cannot explore here. Because of its long history (about 1500 years) it carries with it a great tradition; it also uniquely speaks to God. When we sing psalms and antiphons in this tradition we are reflecting on the words, allowing the music to interpret the words and we are directing this to God. It is a community experience, not an individual experience and it takes into itself the complex relationships in the community between the choir master (often called the Precentor), the cantors who generally have good voices and can lead the singing, and the rest of the community who can contribute very well to the singing because of their long experience of it and their willingness to try. The Chant, and the whole experience of singing offices in choir can be seen as a parable of monastic community life. It builds community, helps to form the character of the monk or nun, offers worship to God and draws visitors into this common prayer.

Music is a very important part of human life and the ubiquitous iPhone or other personal music player shows how many people today spend their time listening to music. The sadness of this is that they only listen. They do not make it. They listen to it in a solitary way, through earphones; they are not drawn into company with others by external performers. People today do not usually make music together even in the simple way of singing together. As high quality music is so easy to produce electronically there is less and less reason to learn to play instruments oneself. Our experience in the monastery suggests people would improve their mental health, get on better together and have a lot of fun if they found ways of singing or playing musical instruments, even badly. Try it and see!

4. Vowed for Life

We live in a very fluid world. In the past people tended to have jobs for life. Now it is common to change jobs every few years. Marriages break up more frequently. People don't want life-long commitments and so have temporary relationships. Against this the religious life expects men and women to commit themselves for life. To say this is against the culture of the age is perhaps an exaggeration. Society would still like marriages to be life long. Society still hankers after stability. Yet the idea of young men and women committing themselves for life to a religious community fills many with horror. People often ask whether temporary commitments are possible.

Actually they are. There are orders which only have temporary arrangements. Also, in traditional communities there is a long period of preparation for life vows. The first period as a novice usually lasts about two years. Then the person takes temporary promises usually for three years, sometimes renewable. It is only after six or eight years that vows are taken for life. And Church law insists that there must be a process available to release people from life vows if they do not work. Yet the ideal remains that we offer our lives to God for life. God is faithful and trustworthy and will not let us down. So life vows are actually a statement of trust in God. Yet, as with marriage, vows and the life which follows do not simply happen. They have to be worked at and we need to understand what they are really about. Although they seem at first sight to be largely geared towards monks and nuns they turn out to have significance for all who are trying to live life well.

People think of the religious vows as those of poverty, chastity and obedience. These are indeed the vows taken by most communities founded since the Thirteenth Century. Benedictine monks and nuns, however, take vows of Stability, Conversion of Life and Obedience. Naturally, poverty and chastity come into this, but the three vows, as we have them, point in a different direction: in different ways they speak of a commitment to live the whole of one's life in this monastic state, seeking the will of God.

a) Stability

Stability describes the commitment to be a nun or monk of one particular monastery. Joining a monastery is rather like being born into a family. We have only one family and cannot change families at will. If family relationships are to be real we need to spend time with each other. We can't simply go off on our own jaunts whenever we like. Some monasteries have a strict rule of enclosure and members hardly ever leave the monastic precincts. This is not a negative reaction to the world, nor is it an attempt to create a prison. 'Stone walls do not a prison make, nor iron bars a cage.'[13] This kind of stability makes it possible to dig deep into the life of prayer, to build up resources both of individuals and community which others can draw on. Our society is a very mobile society and lacks roots. Society needs people who stay in one place, as they tend to do when they have bought their own properties. So, too, monasteries give the Church places of quiet and calm, places where pools are deep. Nuns and monks called to this life do not usually feel trapped. From a very small geographical base one is free to roam through infinity in mind and spirit.[14]

---

[13] Richard Lovelace *To Althea, from Prison*

[14] A lovely fifteenth century carol describes Jesus himself beautifully: 'Heaven and earth in little space, res miranda *(a wonderful thing).'*

Some monastic communities do have an outside ministry, involving parish, or mission work. Balancing their external commitments with this essential stability can be a real difficulty, but the principle remains the same. God has called us to this life and it is our knowledge of God's love for us which keeps us bound to it.

C.S. Lewis once wrote of a stable which 'had something inside it that was bigger than the whole world.'[15] In that way a monastery reverses the time and space that we know. Physically, it covers only a small patch of ground. Physically, the nuns or monks inside may seem to be imprisoned in a small space, yet their experience of this small space will be quite different from how it seems. It will range through time, both through the centuries behind and the unknown time ahead. It will range through space to the peoples all over the earth. And it will share in the life of God, so participating in infinity. That actually is what all Christian life does; if we can see it in a monastery, we see it happening more clearly in the rest of the world.

"Why do you stand looking into heaven?"[16]

If you stand still on a busy pavement in town and look up in the sky you will get a number of different reactions. Some will walk round you; some will bump into you; some will be rude to you. Some will stop and look up into the sky to see what you are looking at: an aeroplane, a beautiful cloud formation, or maybe even someone hanging from a window. The more people stop and look, the more other people will stop and look. That is not a bad parable of the role of monastic communities.

---

[15] C.S.Lewis, *The Last Battle,* the final book of *The Chronicles of Narnia.*
[16] Acts 1:11

Society has often looked on monastics as a waste of time and space. Some governments have closed down monasteries, accusing them of being parasites. Some rulers, like Henry VIII, accused them of hoarding the nation's wealth (which he wanted). Monasteries seem to be hangovers from the past, obstacles to developing a new society open to the needs of the modern age. It is not only those hostile to Christianity who think this of monasteries. So do many Christians. They accuse us of being wrapped up in ourselves, seeking our own salvation, contemplating our navels and being 'so heavenly minded, they are no earthly use.' In a Church which is declining in numbers and deeply concerned to bring new people into the Christian faith can we really afford these men and women stuck away in their monasteries? Or indeed, in a world that is falling apart, fractured by injustice and shot through with disaster, do we not need Christians who will go out into the world with the message of Christ and the modern miracles of healing, development aid and social concern and change the world? Monasteries are a luxury we cannot afford. Historically, of course, there is some truth in this. At various times in the past monasteries became very wealthy and became identified with the rich and powerful segments of society oppressing the poor. This is hardly the case now. But are we too concerned for ourselves?

St Ignatius of Loyola began the Spiritual Exercises with the statement: 'Man is created to praise, reverence and serve God our Lord, and by this means to save his soul.' At first sight that does look as if we exist simply to worship God and save ourselves. In fact, Ignatius founded the Jesuits who have always been intensely involved in the world, teaching, preaching, running parishes and missions, studying, getting engaged with social justice and even being martyred in civil wars.[17] Serving God and loving God should make us intensely aware of how much God cares for the other people on earth. We have to ask ourselves often, "What are we doing for the people God loves?"

Some monasteries are directly involved in such work as teaching in schools, running parishes or even doing development work in the Third World. That is important work but they need to keep in mind that this is not their main reason for existing. We exist for God. We are like the men and women standing on a pavement looking up to heaven. The world needs to acknowledge God, to turn its attention to him and to be taken up with his glory. This is not for his sake. God doesn't need us; nor does he need our praise. We need him, and if we are to grow up healthy and wise we need to be turned towards him as a sunflower is turned towards the sun. The majority of our society probably won't do this as they are unaware of God, or too busy, or can't see the point of it. Even some who would love to do it because they do love God simply do not have the time. So monks and nuns do it on their behalf.

All Christians do this too. People often mock the church because 'it is full of grey haired men and women.' Yet these grey haired men and women keep the churches open till others need them. They meet Sunday by Sunday praying for the world and offering the worship that helps direct the world back to God. A priest saying mass is not simply indulging a private devotion, or ministering to the needs of those in

---

[17] I think here particularly of Martin Thomas, John Conway, Christopher Shepherd-Smith and Gerry Pieper whom I knew and who were martyred along with others in Zimbabwe

church. He is offering the most powerful intercession on behalf of the world, offering the sacrifice which Christ offered on the Cross for the salvation of the world. A small group of people, with or without their priest, saying evensong together are praying in the Body of Christ for everyone living around them. What we do in our monasteries they do in their churches. We are one in this work.

People visit us: some are devout Christians seeking to know God more. Many are troubled people looking for advice and help. People come delivering groceries, or to fix the plumbing or to offer some of the many services that connect us with society. Are they influenced by us? Do they discover new values or new beliefs because of us? For the most part we simply do not know. It is not for us to know how God uses us in other people's lives. For the most part it is better we don't know. If we did know we might think it was due to our cleverness or goodness. In fact, it is only due to God. We do believe, though, that our contacts with all kinds of people, our prayers for them and the world and our function of standing still looking up into heaven has a role in the mission of the Church and the coming of the Kingdom of God which may actually be more important than the more obvious active roles. We may turn a common saying on its head: "Don't just do something; stand there!" In an over active, over busy and confused world we need some people who will simply stand still.

b) Conversion of Life

The Latin phrase for this is not easy to translate: *Conversatio Morum.* It seems not to mean conversion in the sense of a religious conversion where one moves from one state of belief to another. It is in fact more like a conversation with life. Day by day we have to see how our life needs to change, to grow and to take on new information. In that sense it is like any normal human life growing as the family grows, the work responsibility grows and the world around us changes. Yet for monks and nuns much of this will be to do with the relationships we live with. They make a constant demand on us. We see in Christian terms that jealousy, envy, bad temper and selfishness are destructive to those around us and also to ourselves. We think we have overcome these sins but find them resurfacing. We find them appearing in new forms. We also see more and more that what we might call our spiritual life, that is the life of prayer, is actually bound up with everything we do in life. It can't be neatly separated out. If we want to listen properly to God we have to listen to other people.

As we live our monastic life we realise more and more how our attitudes need to be deeply changed away from the self-centredness which is natural to human beings. Yet we are not the only ones who must learn this. Christians who begin to take their faith seriously will find themselves constantly out of step with society. Even those who have no Christian faith realise that, if we are to save the environment, or help the poor, or trade responsibly with oppressive regimes we need to think of others more than ourselves.

To take one example, many of us grew up in an environment where racism was endemic. This is not just in places like South Africa but in many communities in the UK. Racist jokes, racist attitudes and assumptions about people of colour are simply a natural part of life's fabric. Many will deny this because they haven't seen how deep the racist attitudes go. Others who think they have seen it and been converted away from it will be shocked from time to time to realise some remnants of this racism still remain. When one discovers this it is not just a matter for guilt or breast beating; it is even a matter of thanksgiving that some other fault deep within us has been revealed and can now be dealt with. God doesn't expect us to be perfect in this life. He knows better than anyone our imperfect natures. He does expect us to try to discover how our lives need changing and to do what we can to put those changes into affect. That is conversion of life.

There are no simple rules about this; no neat formulae. It is a matter of attending every day to the Spirit of God (or one's own awareness of the world around us) and trying to follow up the little hints and movements that slowly and steadily turn us into the people God wants us to be. It is really the working out of the commitment to stability. Staying in one place we have the chance to see more clearly what we need to do to grow.

c) Obedience

I once met a delightful old nun in Germany who had grown up under the Nazi regime. She described how, as a seventeen year old sheltering from the bombs raining down on Würzburg she had promised, "If I survive this I must give my life to God." She did survive, and the next question was how to do it. She then decided to join a Sisterhood because "Nazism had so corrupted the idea of obedience, I needed to show others what obedience is really about."

Obedience brings to mind the heel clicking obedience of the army or maybe the training of dogs. In past times children were expected to be constantly obedient to their parents and servants to their masters. Monks and nuns were obedient to the superiors. Obedience made for a well functioning society. It was also a cause of much abuse.

Today we understand obedience better. The word itself comes from the Latin word *audio* meaning 'I hear'. Obedience is about listening and the listening needs to be mutual. This is common advice in the workplace, not just in the monastery. If a Superior wants to ask a monk to do something he needs to explain why. He needs also to have got to know the person to know whether he really has the skills or personality for the job. He must listen to the monk's reaction. He may still ask him to do it but he must listen before insisting.

Likewise, the monk himself must listen to his Superior. He will have his reasons for asking. A job needs to be done and no one else can do it. Once the monk has understood that he may be more willing to agree.

St Benedict emphasises over and over again that monks must be obedient. That is at the heart of monastic life. He gives a whole chapter to the subject of obedience, how it needs to be instant and full hearted. Yet towards the end of the Rule he moderates this and says that a monk who genuinely feels he cannot do what was asked of him should put his case 'without pride, obstinacy or refusal.'[18] He may still have to do it 'trusting in God's help', and then the challenge will be for him to do it in love. As in any marriage, or any relationship, love changes the nature of obedience from something we have to do, to something we really want to do.

Military obedience can teach the rest of us something important. In combat, soldiers can't be stopping constantly to discuss whether the

---

[18] RB 68:3

latest command really is the best for the circumstances. They have to trust the officer and get on and do it. Trust is built up in training. Soldiers discover the officer really cares about them and won't sacrifice their lives if he can help it. They learn whether his judgement is good and whether he knows what he is doing. Then they will trust him. Officers have to work hard to gain that trust. This is true in monasteries, in families, in industry or in any aspect of daily life. The right kind of obedience simplifies life and makes it run smoothly, but it is founded on trust. It isn't rocket science: there are no neat formulae and anyone can understand it. Obedience simply has to be worked for. In the modern world we look for instant answers to our questions. Real answers take time to emerge and time to establish themselves. That is where obedience, listening and stability come in.

5. Silence

Many years ago when I was living in Johannesburg I flew up to Zimbabwe for a visit. Early next morning I took a rural bus out to my former mission station in Chikwaka. Buses in Africa are great fun: people, chickens and babies add their noises to the rattle of the loose bodywork and the roar of the engine. When I got off the bus and began to walk into the bush I was struck by the complete silence around me. Not a noise was to be heard. This, I thought, was the famous silence of the bush. I was wrong. As I walked I became aware of noises: birds tweeting in the trees, voices of local people working in the fields, even the noise of the wind going through the grass and the occasional cricket squeaking. The bush is not silent, but its noises do not disturb you. They are natural and embedded in that world. However, I did realise how I never heard those noises in Johannesburg. I had got so used to blocking out the noise of traffic that I needed time and space to begin to hear again what was really going on around me. Silence is refreshing to our minds as we don't have to spend energy all the time, unconsciously blocking out the noise of daily life in a city.

We live in a noisy world. Traffic sounds are a background to most of our lives. Supermarkets have piped music; so do bus stations and railway stations. If there is no piped music then there are loud announcements. Some trains have Quiet Coaches because the coaches get so noisy with conversation, phones and lap tops that many passengers cannot cope. The only defence against other people's noise is to get ear phones and plug yourself into your own music. It is still noise, but at least it is your own choice.

Churches used to be silent places but this too has often disappeared. People are convinced silence is unfriendly so everyone talks before the service, during it and after. Some brave clergy put up notices like: 'Please talk to God before the service and your neighbour afterwards.' It has little effect and one dare not enforce it for fear of giving offence. Older people believe all this noise has a bad effect on people's hearing, attention span, concern for others and ability to think. Younger people say it is just normal.

When people come into a monastery the first thing that strikes them usually is the silence. Some find it difficult. They certainly need help in keeping it. Yet quite quickly the silence becomes warm and friendly. It allows them space to be themselves. They may first discover how disturbed they are as the silence forces them to notice the turmoil of emotions and thoughts surging through their brains. As the turmoil calms down they begin to discover a space in which they can listen to what is going on inside them. Then they find they can listen to God, and believe God is listening to them. Most first time visitors to a monastery wonder how they will cope with the silence. Most find they don't want it to end when the time comes to leave.

Why is silence so important? What does Benedict have to say about it? He doesn't actually say very much and what he does say is a bit on the negative side. In Ch. 6 he quotes Ps. 39, 'I was silent and was humbled, and I refrained even from good words' and comments, 'Here the Prophet indicates that there are times when good words are to be left unsaid out of esteem for silence. For all the more reason, then, should evil speech be curbed so that punishment for sin may be avoided.'

Benedict, at this stage in the rule is still very suspicious of all speech as tending towards sin. So in the next chapter on humility the monk 'controls his tongue and remains silent…for Scripture warns *in a flood of words you will not avoid sinning.*'[19] In Ch. 38 monks must keep silence in the refectory so as to listen to the reader. This is an obvious courtesy (and it is astonishing how many people today do not think of the discourtesy of making lots of noise in another's presence) but also reminds us that the refectory parallels the church as a place of instruction, reflection and attention to God.

Chapter 42 begins 'Monks should diligently cultivate silence at all times, but especially at night.' Obviously this is to get on with the business of sleeping, and that priority is reinforced here by the instruction for a few pages of something beneficial to be read to them after supper – but nothing too exciting like Old Testament history books which may keep the brothers awake! And in Ch. 52 the monks are told to leave the church 'in complete silence…so that a brother who may wish to pray alone will not be disturbed by the insensitivity of another.'

Benedict is right in all that he says about silence. Unthinking chatter does lead to sin. St James famously describes the tongue as the most dangerous member of the body[20] and monks and nuns know how true this is. Talkative people can also be very dominating, even self centred. The phrase about 'trying to get a word in edgeways' reveals the exasperation most of us feel in the face of other people's talk. But what

---

[19] RB7:57 and Ps. 10

[20] James 3:6-8 'The tongue is a fire, a world of evil. Placed among the parts of our bodies, the tongue contaminates the whole body and sets on fire the course of life, and is itself set on fire by hell. For all kinds of animals, birds, reptiles, and sea creatures can be or have been tamed by humans, but no one can tame the tongue. It is an uncontrollable evil filled with deadly poison.'

of our own? One of our most delightful but exasperating brethren was once said to “keep on talking while he thought of something to say.” Most of us could profitably talk less, and certainly in places like the church one needs a good reason to talk at all.

Yet none of this really speaks of the attractiveness of silence to those of us who live in it, or choose to visit it. St Benedict, of course, lived in a world where almost the only noise was the human voice. Radio, TV, phones, cars, trains and all the other noises which pollute our lives did not yet exist. He valued silence but had not yet come to realise the dangers of noise created by things other than tongues.

Monasteries are not completely silent places. Apart from the worship in church, there is frequent need to talk, in teaching, counselling, business and common chat. Even in times when total silence is supposed to prevail, such as at night or in retreat, there are many legitimate occasions to break it – when caring for the sick for instance. Silence needs to be guarded and cherished. It is a wonderful gift which we can share with our visitors. It must not be allowed to become selfish (“my silence!”). Charity always trumps rules of silence. Yet even the extroverts among us value the silence. Coming back from a journey out into what is sometimes referred to as the ‘real world’, most of us feel relieved to step back into monastic silence. This is more real.

Recently, my niece got married and she and her new husband (both in media work) went off to a Pacific island for their honeymooon, leaving all screens behind. They loved this freedom from electronic communication. Now a few days ‘digital detox’ has become a regular feature of their lives. Similarly, when people come to Mirfield for retreats we often invite them to hand in their phones. Those who have the courage to do so always find it a liberation. It is simply not true that the world, or their family needs them to be instantly available. They really do need time to discover themselves.

A request for silence can seem selfish. In our current noisy world it seems someone wants to opt out of relationship. He or she wants to impose his minority will on others who enjoy the noise. This assumes the majority do like the noise. In fact they may not, but have been conditioned not to complain. More deeply though silence can be seen as an act of generosity to other people's needs. Considering the other's needs is fundamental to Christianity; it also fundamental to a smoothly operating society. A supermarket chain in England has one day a week when no background music is played in their stores. This is to enable autistic people, who find such music intolerable, to go shopping. Autistic people are a small minority of the population so it is really good that this supermarket is willing to consider their needs. It would be quite a change in our inherently selfish culture if those who use mobile phones could consider the needs and comfort of those sitting near them!

Silence actually helps us to get to know each other on a deeper level. I was once on a retreat with a number of German Sisters. One alienated us from the start; she was loud, aggressive and clearly had no time for priests. I was glad to escape into silence away from her. Yet as the retreat went on I got to know her more deeply, through intercessions she offered and little things I noticed. She had been in Berlin as a nurse when the Russians arrived in 1945. She had worked for years in tough mission hospitals, perhaps with bullying priests. She had a crooked back and was in pain. Inside this hard, aggressive exterior was a sensitive wounded person trying to get out. Only in the silence could I have discovered that.

6. Prayer

a) Liturgy

Some years ago in London a seventeen year old boy was wandering back from a party late on Christmas Eve when he saw lights on in a church. Intrigued, he went in and found himself at Midnight Mass. He was entranced by the beauty of the liturgy. When others went up to Communion he did as well. That started him on a journey into faith which led him ten years later to abandon a successful career as an accountant and become a priest.

At roughly the same time as this young man went to Midnight Mass a young Romanian in Timisoara set off to a rock concert in the central park. When he got there he found there was no rock concert. The park is next to Timisoara's magnificent cathedral and Constantine decided to go in and look around. This was in Communist times and he had no Christian training. He went in and found the evening service in progress. He was overwhelmed by its beauty and its sense of the transcendent. During the week that followed he tried to convince himself it was all rubbish, but he went back and again was amazed. So it went on for several weeks until he finally approached a priest and asked to talk. He too is now a priest.

Liturgy is not an automatic tool of conversion. Some are bored by it, or find it beautiful but irrelevant. Some like it rich and exotic. Others prefer an utter simplicity. Yet over and over again in the history of our church one finds people stepping into a church service and being changed by it. This should not surprise us. What does surprise us is that it happens at services we ourselves are celebrating, often rather badly.

Of course it is not because we do it well that people are necessarily touched by God. God himself is present in the liturgy and will touch those who are open to being touched. It is a mystery why some are touched and others not; this makes us wonder at the mysterious activity of God. We can't use liturgy to manipulate people. We can't overawe them in order to force their conversion. Liturgy keeps us humble. We can only offer it to God in the best way we can and let Him do the work with those who come into it. It is not we who are doing the liturgy who convert the unwary stranger. It is God who is able to touch some and not others. Mission has mystery at its very heart and so does the liturgy.

Good liturgy speaks for itself. It speaks of God. It is largely made up of Scripture and prayers clearly directed to God. Good liturgy is also rich in symbols. Music, vestments, movement and the church building itself all have things to say to the people taking part. What they say is often on an unconscious level. Sometimes it is good to explain what is going on. Sometimes it is not. Liturgy should not be dumbed-down or over-explained or it becomes a patronising lesson and excludes God.

One of the really important characteristics of liturgy is that it is communal. The visitor is welcomed into a group of Christians. They share their faith with him or her simply by being there and taking part. As a community they show the promise of what is to come. Christians can never be isolated believers. They are part of the Body of Christ. A person coming into this community must know that these could be his brothers and sisters, and like them he could become a citizen of the Kingdom of Heaven, a fellow citizen in the household of God[21].

---

[21] Ephesians 2:19

Liturgy can also help us overcome one of the big problems of evangelisation: who is it aimed at? If you direct it to only one group such as the young, lots of other groups are left out. If you aim it at children, adults will quickly get bored since it does not touch the real problems of life. (So will the children get bored if they are stuck with endless choruses and simplistic bible tales, but that's another story.) Liturgy properly presented really can be all-age worship, mixed-ability learning. The symbols speak to everyone. Traditional hymns have good tunes but also good theology that can engage the thinking minds. It is fun for the children to dress up, carry candles and swing a thurible. At the same time anyone with a real ability to think and investigate will find the liturgy a huge treasure-chest of theology and Christian history. Parts of it go back to the time of Christ. Different cultures and languages have left their mark. The biblical readings themselves cover the whole story of salvation over the course of a year and are an excellent syllabus for teaching. Layer upon layer waits to be unpeeled and absorbed.

In communist countries no teaching of the Christian faith was allowed, outside a few monasteries or seminaries. Nothing was taught in school. Yet when communism collapsed it was astonishing how much people still knew about their faith in countries like Romania and Russia where they had, sometimes, been allowed to go to church. Just standing there in the liturgy, often celebrated in a language they didn't understand, they absorbed the central truths of Christian life. Even without the church liturgy, during the darkest days, icons, service books, simple prayers at home kept bringing new generations into faith in Christ. Liturgy carries the faith down the centuries of history. That is what monasteries do as well. Parish churches, if well looked after tell the same story. There is no need to keep inventing new wheels for evangelism. The ones we have, properly used, work very well.

b) Daily Office

When you go into a monastic service you meet a kind of worship that hardly exists elsewhere anymore, except in Cathedrals. It is not performed for a congregation. Its purpose is not to entertain, instruct, or exhort the people. It is primarily offered to God. The music helps to make this clear. It is the timeless music of plainsong which gathers up the worship of nearly two thousand years. We become part of a great company of men and women worshipping God over the ages, and over space and time.

We do this because we need it. That is what brought us into the monastery. Like the sun flower we know our need to keep ourselves turned toward the sun. We do it for the world as well. We don't just intercede for the world, praying for the sick, for governments, for peace; we pray on behalf of the world. We offer the praise that people in society do not offer, either because they have no time, or because they aren't aware that they need to. We believe that our prayer and praise helps to turn society that little bit more in the direction of God. Other people think we do that too; that is why they give us gifts of money and leave us legacies. That is one of the ways we earn our keep.

We are not alone in this. Clergy of Anglican and Roman Catholic churches are bound by the Church to say morning and evening prayer in some form or another. This is partly for their own good. Priests who give up their regular prayers through laziness or busy-ness generally show it by breaking down, or becoming ineffective. It is also the prayer of the Church offered for the world. It is something priests are paid to do: offer praise, adoration, confession and intercession for all people, Christian or not.

What does this prayer consist of? It is almost entirely Scripture. Much of it is psalms. It includes the canticles from the Old and New Testament. Some of this is praise; some is history, telling about the great works of salvation God has done, especially that of choosing Israel (and then us Christians) for a special role in his drama of salvation. Some of it is complaint. This surprises some people, but it is honest. The Jews in old times were great complainers. They respected God. They sometimes loved him. But if they thought he had got things wrong they were not slow to tell him.

We Christians have inherited that attitude. It shows a confidence in God's love for us. We don't have to be nice to him always. He wants us to be honest, then he can use our honesty to try and explain to us what is really going on. The psalms help us come to God in almost any situation. Sometimes it is sorrow for our sin. Sometimes we are angry because of the way refugees are being treated, and we find the Israelites were refugees and sang psalms about it. Sometimes we are joyful in the presence of God; sometimes we just want to praise him for the good things that have come into our lives. In the Office we do not choose which psalms to sing; we identify with the feelings and thoughts of the psalms and that way we share in the feelings of other people in those situations. That must be prayer, for them and with them.

And as well as the psalms there are long readings from Scripture – history, prophecy and teaching from Old and New Testaments are read to us every day, soaking us in the words of God. The soaking doesn't always work! All of us sometimes seem to be wearing rain coats and fail to take this in. It is possible to sing a whole office and realise one has hardly noticed a word. To some extent that doesn't matter. It is a bit like being on a train; it takes you where you want to go whether you think about it or not. But it is better to think about it if we can; as St Benedict says, 'sing the psalms in such a way that our minds are in harmony with our voices.'[22]

All this is the Opus Dei, 'the Work of God'. But does that mean the work God wants us to do, or the work we do for God? It makes good sense both ways. This is our work. We don't only pray when we feel like it. We pray at set times every day whether we like it or not. We also don't choose our prayer. Our culture today is obsessed with choice. People choose how to worship God. If it doesn't make them feel good they abandon it and try something else. This is very self-centred. Prayer is not intended to make us 'feel good'. We nuns and monks simply get on with doing this work that needs to be done, like the washing up, or the writing of letters. Sometimes we love it. Sometimes we are bored with it, but we get on and do it.

However, we don't work alone. This is also God working. How he does it is his business; we usually don't know. People come to our services and go away feeling encouraged, strengthened, sometimes even converted. It can't be us who have done this. It is God. Does our prayer help to turn the area we are in a little bit towards God? Does the sorrow we sing of help sinners to repent? Does our anger, our sense of

[22] RB 19:7

desperation ("How long O God, will you forget me, forever?"[23]) help the refugees in the Middle East, or in Africa? We don't know. We believe it does because God is with us, and his Holy Spirit is present in our prayer. Our prayer takes place within the Body of Christ and Christ is present throughout the world. Chaos theory says a butterfly flaps its wings in Tokyo and a storm happens in New York. Perhaps our prayer is like that, somehow providing a vehicle for God to do astonishing things all over the world. We just do not know!

c) Private Prayer

In one important sense there is no such thing as private prayer for Christians. We all exist in the Body of Christ. Our prayer is part of that Body and we share it with our fellow Christians. When we pray for each other we pray for people who share the same blood stream as ourselves. So when we talk about private prayer we are thinking of the prayer that goes on inside our heads, particularly when we are alone. Often, when I have to talk to people about prayer I ask whether any of them have problems with prayer. Slowly a few hands go up. Then I put my own hand up. They are astonished! Me, a priest and a monk, how can I have problems with prayer? Well, I do and so do all people who pray. When we have problems it may be because we are lazy, or sinful. It is much more likely to be because we are human. Prayer can be difficult, but if we look at the difficulties we can discover more about prayer.

a) The first problem most people have is 'distractions'; that is, the mind wanders. All sorts of irrelevant ideas come into our heads. We are trying to talk to God, or think about God and we

[23] Psalm 13

find ourselves remembering conversations from the previous day, or planning what to have for lunch. This is normal. Our brains are constantly active. We can't switch them off. If we did we would be dead. I find there are two useful ways of dealing with distractions. One is to think of them as prayer: people we are worrying about, situations that are difficult need to be prayed for, so when they appear in our prayer we can just refer them to God. That is good quality intercession.

A second way is to see the distraction as a temptation to turn away from God. So we can use it to turn back to God. Each time we turn our attention back to God we are saying "God, you are more important to me than this memory." That in itself is a good thing to do and really is prayer.

b) A second difficulty we have in today's culture is to think that prayer must always be a 'good experience'. Prayer is simply about living in the presence of God. Sometimes it will be happy; there will be moments of joy. Sometimes it will be sad as the sadnesses of our life overwhelm us. Sometimes it will be boring when we are tired, or nothing seems to be happening. The important thing is that we are simply there, in the presence of God. His Holy Spirit will be working with us even if we don't know it. Like children in front of their father or mother, it is enough to be there. Parents don't need to be talked to all the time. Children don't need to perform all the time. Good parents are glad to know that the children can relax in their company. That is prayer.

Psalm 131 is a good example of peaceful, trusting prayer:

O LORD, my heart is not lifted up,
my eyes are not raised too high;
I do not occupy myself with things too great
and too marvellous for me.
But I have calmed and quieted my soul,
like a child quieted at its mother's breast;
like a child that is quieted is my soul.

c) That reminds us of the third important point: we are not here to perform; we don't have to impress God with great thoughts, or wonderful speeches. We need to show that we trust God enough to relax in his presence and tell him anything that is on our minds. Or if we want simply to rest in his presence and say nothing much that too is good. If we want to read a little Scripture and reflect on it in his presence, that is prayer. Prayer simply shows that we trust our heavenly Father and are glad to be with Him. It is not really at all difficult!

7. Order and Balance

Every novice who has joined a monastery has been frustrated by the customs of the house! Sometimes they are given to you as a long list of rules. Sometimes they are not told to you; you just stumble over them and get rebuked. Many seem pointless, or petty. Some *are* pointless and petty. But they are essential to the life of the monastery. Thinking about them often reveals important clues to understanding the life.

The great Cistercian Order used to have a single customary comprised of over 600 customs observed in every house everywhere in the world. Some years ago, these rules were set aside and houses were told to make up their own. Monks in the Cistercian order stand to sing the psalms so when they stand up they lift up their hinged seats so they can lean gently against them. One rule had decreed that when monks stood up in choir to sing they should raise their seats with their right hands. Now they could use either hand. Immediately, they found the reason for the original rule: in a closely packed choir they kept banging each other with their knuckles when they used different hands!

Many of the rules we keep are simply pragmatic. It is important in a house with many people that everyone knows where everything is. Any cook knows what a nuisance it is when someone else comes into the kitchen and helpfully tidies things away. It can be weeks before the wooden spoons are found again! So in church, in the sacristy, in the refectory, or anywhere else there is a place where things must stay. The place is often random (though most often it does make sense) but it mustn't change. Keeping these rules is not just a matter of rule keeping. It has its significance in mutual love. Sensitivity to each other is a key element of Benedict's Rule. Christian love is not just a high ideal. It has very down-to-earth, practical consequences. Making sure that pots and pans are in their right place is one way we show consideration for our brothers and sisters.

At another level, rules often have good reasons behind them: in our community there is a rule not to talk when clearing the tables after a meal. If people talk they often stand still and block the gangway so that others can't get on with clearing. Or, if they talk while clearing they are soon shouting down the length of the table which is disruptive. Likewise, there is a rule which says only one person from a table should clear away the first course. If more than one person does it, a scrum forms as too many people try to put things on the trolley.

The levels of significance can rise: we have a rule that says 'No talking in church.' How else can the church be kept as a place of prayer? Another custom says that brethren should enter choir from the side aisles, and never walk across the gap of about fifteen feet in the centre of choir. The first part of this custom ensures that decorum is maintained as people slip into choir with the least amount of disturbance. Not walking across the centre of choir preserves a sense of sacred space. If the centre of choir and the sanctuary round the altar are kept sacred and only entered when really necessary, they become places where God's presence can reside. People often comment on the wonderful sense of prayer, and the presence of God, which our church has. Rules like this keep that safe.

At yet another level, rules have an important function helping us to grow in the Christian life. All of us are self-centred. As Christians, especially as nuns or monks, we find we spend our whole life trying to grow out of self-centredness. St Francis de Sales said that self-centredness dies half an hour after we do. Living together in a community is supposed to accelerate this process. It should knock jagged corners off brothers and sisters, make them more aware of each other's needs, making them even want to do things for others that may inconvenience themselves. Rules help us to do this. A rule telling us not to play our radios after compline (our final act of worship before we go to bed) is not just intended to keep the Night Silence of the monastery; it lets other people go to sleep. Self-will is the biggest enemy of Christian life. It needs to be constantly opposed. The Orthodox have a phrase about 'cutting the will.' That sounds a bit radical but every rule or custom that we learn to keep, preferably willingly, has the effect of cutting back that self-will.

Rules do not only apply to monastic life. We need rules in society. Some of these are enshrined in law – in our present day parliaments spend a lot of time making rules that aim (and fail) to give us a perfectly regulated society. There are unspoken rules which should help us to think of other people. Rules help us to see the bigger picture which with our tunnel vision we do not normally appreciate. Playing loud music late at night can disturb the neighbours, waking their children and leaving all of them tired and irritated the next day. Making rules for ourselves about what to buy and how to live will help us preserve the environment and lessen the destructive impact we are having on poor people in other parts of the world.

Rhythm or balance is one of the qualities that visitors seem to value in the life we lead in the monastery. Days are long and the life is demanding. We have few days off, little time off, and yet we do not break down. People find nuns and monks mostly relaxed, well integrated people. How do they manage it? It is largely because the rhythm of prayer, work, meals and recreation keep us well balanced. By contrast, life in the secular world tends to be very irregular, with long, exhausting hours of work, irregular meals, and forms of recreation which tend to involve even more activity, and do not really give the body and mind time to rest. Yet, we need to remember that monastic life is not essentially a society for healthy living. It is a life centred on God and God wants us to live life to the full. The structure we have evolved makes that possible. It should prevent us from being self-indulgent, self-centred in our concern for our own comfort. Human sin, of course, can frustrate even this good intent.

We also have to remember that some rules or customs do become pointless. We stick to them out of pig-headedness, determined not to change. A novice once asked me if he could move a rubbish bin in the kitchen. Certainly not, I thought. Don't let this whippersnapper change things! Then he pointed out no one used it where it was and the space it was taking up could accommodate a small fridge that *was* needed. He was right, of course. It is quite easy to find ourselves serving the rules rather than letting the rules serve us. Jesus warned us of that danger when he said, "The Sabbath was made for man, not man for the Sabbath."[24]

---

[24] Mark 2:27

8. Identity: The Habit

One of our brethren was once in a supermarket wearing his habit when a boy came up to him and said “Are you a nun?” “No,” he said. “I’m a monk.” “So, are you married to a nun?”

The clothes we wear in monastic life do excite considerable fascination. Why do we wear them? This question is a little complicated by the fact that so many sisters, brothers and religious priests have given up wearing any sort of habit. Why do some of us stick to ours?

First, one needs to be clear: it is not the habit that makes a monk. You can be a deeply devout and very committed monk or nun without a habit. People have to live without habits sometimes in times of persecution. Those religious who do not wear habits are not necessarily less good religious than those who do. It is true, however, that those now who do wear habits tend to be on the monastic side of the spectrum. We need to account for our choice.

In the first place, habits are a form of identity. Each community or congregation has its own particular style. Having identity is important in life. It helps us to know who we are trying to be. A habit reminds us all the time that we have chosen a life which is full time. We have to live it every day, all day. There is no time off. A habit also sets us apart, not as special Christians but as different Christians. That helps to remind us of the way we should live, think and speak.

Habits also link us to the past. Our clothes are not exactly those of any century but they do bear a likeness to what people wore in the middle ages. Monastic life does not live in the past but it is very conscious of its long history. It is like a river which has flowed for 1700 years or more.

Much of its wisdom comes from the past, and we are not ashamed of that. Monastic life has a sense of Catholic tradition which reminds people that the boundaries of our lives are very narrow if we keep them wholly in the present. Christians are members of the Body of Christ which makes us concerned for other Christians all over the world, and connects us with Christians in the past as well. To be Catholic is to have a very wide stage on which to live, and habits remind us of that.

Habits are also a sign of poverty, or simplicity. Many schools like their children to wear school uniforms so that all are dressed the same; rich and poor kids are not distinguished by their dress. There is less opportunity for children to show off their clothes, or despise others for theirs. So, too, with us. Habits tell us we are all brothers or sisters, all equal, all possessing the same rights, all part of the same family. They save us a lot of money, too, as a habit lasts for years and we do not need often to spend money on clothes. That applies to those of us also who do sometimes wear mufti. Most of us do not have very posh-looking clothes. Some brothers look notoriously like tramps when they go out for a walk!

Habits save a lot of time. Jesus himself speaks of the tyranny of the question, what shall we wear?[25] We don't have to bother about that in the morning. Habits also function anywhere, on a walk, in our rooms, at the pub or even on a visit to Buckingham Palace, though one might put on a clean one for that!

Habits can also tell a story that is significant in the development of a particular Religious Community.

---

[25] Luke 12:22

The development of the Habit of the Community of the Resurrection, by Fr Nicolas

Our CR habit is a double-breasted cassock with a leather belt, a cross which is unique to CR and a grey scapular. When CR started in 1892, English people were very suspicious of monks. Even Roman Catholic monks tended not to wear habits in public. English people thought we might be Romish agents wanting to steal away the good Protestant souls of this island. For that reason we wore a double-breasted cassock and a belt just like most parish priests. After about 20 years, we decided to add to this a badge, which turned into a cross with the crucifix on one side and the Lamb and Flag, a symbol of the Resurrection, on the other. Another twenty years passed before some brethren returned from Africa wearing scapulars. They tried to convince the other brethren that these were very convenient, keeping cassocks clean, but failed. They were told to remove them. Despite that, scapulars soon became part of the dress, but were regarded as aprons. They could only be worn in the house or in the grounds; never in church and never outside the grounds. Another fifty years had to pass before scapulars were accepted as part of our habit to be worn everywhere except, curiously enough, in our coffins!

For the Stanbrook community of nuns the Habit also tells an important tale, by Sr Philippa

Our community lived at Cambrai in the Low Countries from 1623 until 1793 when they were arrested and imprisoned by the French

Revolutionaries[26]. They were forced to abandon their habits and wore instead secular clothes belonging to their Carmelite fellow-prisoners who were guillotined. The nuns arrived back in England in 1795, reduced in numbers, in poor health and poverty-stricken, to live in a series of borrowed houses, more or less like pious ladies, until in 1838 a couple of monk friends purchased Stanbrook House, Worcester on their behalf. It was several decades before there was any hope of restoring the enclosure or the religious habit.

Eventually, under the leadership of a French abbess Gertude, assisted by Fr Laurence Shepherd, an Ampleforth monk, we were able to build a proper monastery with a monastic church and to re-establish the enclosure, including parlours with grilles – and to return to wearing the full monastic habit. Abbess Gertrude wrote to her great friend, Mère Cecile Bruyere, abbess of Solesmes, for the pattern of their habits, which we have been wearing ever since with small modifications. Interestingly, there seems to have been much more French influence upon our life in the late 19th century in England than there ever had been when we were resident in Cambrai.

It may seem very odd that we in the 21st century are wearing what is more or less medieval attire, but there are many advantages. It is definitely not 'in fashion' – and therefore never out of fashion; it is timeless. Wearing the habit in some contexts has led me to be charged with 'power dressing!' For example it provides free entrance to the numerous monastic buildings of the country – from the great cathedrals to the ruins of Byland and Rievaulx.

26 This story is movingly told by Dame Anne Teresa Partington in *The Benedictine Dames of Cambray*. Available from Stanbrook Abbey.

Again, it is never out-of-place, though on occasion it can raise an eye-brow. It looks dignified and graceful – and covers a multitude of defects! It also permits of numerous extra layers underneath, for those who suffer from the cold, and is loose enough to be comfortable for those who suffer from the heat. Wearing the habit on trains or buses or walking down a city street can lead to many encounters which would not otherwise take place.

Some of these reasons may seem trivial, yet underneath them all is the power of the symbol. Many of today's religious feel, perhaps rightly, that the nature of their work demands them to be as closely identified with the people they serve as possible. Habits seem to cut them off and are therefore dispensed with. Others of us find the habit says a great deal about the nature of the life, set apart for God, participating in an ancient wisdom and with all of us clearly looking the same; equal, at least in principle. Those few young people today who want to try the religious life seem to want the symbols also that will help make such a radical choice. It is hard to break away from a secular culture that has so many other symbols, from electronic devices to fashions of clothing, which bind one to that life. A new way of dressing says it all.

9. Community: Unity in Diversity

People who live outside a monastery often imagine that life in the monastery must be utterly peaceful, full of loving, joyful Christians who never give each other trouble. Sadly, this is not the case. Women and men who live in monasteries are very much like their brothers and sisters outside. They are imperfect, flawed, often sinful human beings who must spend the whole of their monastic life trying to grow into something like the people God intended them to be.

This is not a new problem; it has always been the case, and we see it reflected in Benedict's Rule. Most of the Rule is about quite small things to do with getting on with each other. Chapter 4 on The Tools for Good Works contains seventy-four helpful bits of advice ranging from 'love the Lord your God with all your heart' to 'You are not to act in anger or nurse a grudge… Never give a hollow greeting of peace or turn away when someone needs your love.' This really is the stuff of monastic life. Every day we are dealing with the same people doing the ordinary things that make up human life. Some make unnecessary noise, others leave the top off the cereal packets. One can be totally distracted in choir by a brother who sings flat or irritated because the washing machine is in use when I want it.

St Benedict knew these problems and more. The men who tried to live the monastic life with him were far from perfect. In an early part of his life some of his monks actually tried to poison him! By the time he came to write his rule he had learned to make provision for the imperfections of his brothers. Some of these were so committed to having personal possessions they hid them among their blankets. Many were constantly disobedient. Others couldn't be trusted with authority since they immediately started throwing their weight around, or even stirring up trouble against the Abbot. A few were so stupid, or obstinate they simply had to be beaten to get them to understand. St Benedict is not soft. His discipline can be very firm. He will exclude a monk from conversation with other monks to get him to think about his faults. On occasion he recognises he must simply expel a monk or the community will suffer.

Yet for the most part Benedict exercises patience. People need time to see how their behaviour is wrong; they need time to learn to put it right. Growth in holiness cannot be achieved overnight but is worked on throughout life, slowly and steadily attending to the little things until the faults fall away and patience, generosity and unselfishness take their place. Benedict does not try to force all his monks into one mould of 'the perfect monk.' Some monastic communities have tried to do this and it is always disastrous. People can live an artificial life for a while but then it breaks down in conflicts, in hypocrisy or in major scandals of abuse. Benedict recognises that people have different talents, different characters, different weaknesses and strengths. Monastic superiors need to recognise this and allow their brothers and sisters to find unity within a diversity of common behaviour and love.

In one sense, if they do that they have achieved their purpose. To create a kind of well of even imperfect unity and love in this troubled world is to offer a great gift to the people around us. How many people come to monasteries simply for that sense of quiet peace, space and an unobtrusive care for their needs and their troubles! It is a tough world we live in and people get battered by it. Coming for visits of just a few hours or a few days to a monastic community can be immensely helpful in recovering from this battering and rediscovering one's priorities. Can we go further? Can we believe that these people take something of that peace back into the world from which they come? They too can become small centres of peace and unity in a troubled world. Sometimes monasteries will have formal ways in which people can be helped to do this, by becoming associates of that community and living by a simple rule that helps to put Christian principles into practice in daily life.

And again, we don't stop there. The Christian church is divided. It has always been so. St Paul had to deal with problems in the early churches he founded. In the first centuries parts of the church broke away on account of various doctrinal disputes. In the Eleventh Century the Church split between East and West, and then in the Sixteenth Century the Reformation left behind a host of different churches which we know today. For more than a hundred years the churches have been trying to come together again. It is proving a long and difficult process with differences of doctrine, custom, history and worship all needing to be addressed. Benedict can help us in this process.

In the first place many of the churches today have forms of the religious life. Roman Catholics and Orthodox are well known for their great monasteries and religious orders, but even in the Anglican, Reformed and Lutheran traditions there are religious communities. When we meet together we find that we are united by far more than what divides us. We recognise common vows, a common vocation to serve God, a common experience of what it is like to live in a religious community. We find ourselves reading Scripture in the same way and seeing the one Jesus as the focus of all our lives. All of us are strongly committed to the Christian denominations in which we live and have no wish to leave them, yet all of us see our life as one which prefigures the life of a united Christian body. 'Unity in diversity' has become a phrase that sums up the ideal of a united church. It is one which we live every day.

Secondly, St Benedict himself lived before the major divisions of the church which we know today came into existence. We can all look back to him and his Rule as a source of common inspiration. We have seen, too, how Benedictines helped to form Europe as we know it. Much of what passes for European civilisation is simply Christian civilisation nurtured by Benedictine monks and nuns. The European Union is experiencing all kinds of strains as it attempts to cope together with the common problems of Europe. This has recently been exacerbated by the British desire to leave Europe. How the Benedictine tradition can contribute to the recovery of unity on all these fronts remains to be seen but we believe we can contribute. We need to talk about how this may be so.

Back in 1981 the philosopher Alasdair MacIntyre ended his book *After Virtue* with a prophetic passage: 'It is always dangerous to draw too precise parallels between one historical period and another; and among the most misleading of such parallels are those which have been drawn between our own age in Europe and North America and the epoch in which the Roman Empire declined into the Dark Ages. None the less certain parallels there are. A crucial turning point in that earlier history occurred when men and women of good will turned aside from the task of shoring up the Roman *imperium* and ceased to identify the continuation of civility and moral community with the maintenance of that *imperium*. What they set themselves to achieve instead—often not recognising fully what they were doing—was the construction of new forms of community within which the moral life could be sustained so that both morality and civility might survive the coming ages of barbarism and darkness. If my account of our moral condition is correct [one characterised by moral incoherence and unsettleable moral disputes in the modern world], we ought to conclude that for some time now we too have reached that turning point. What matters at this stage is the construction of local forms of community within which civility and the intellectual and moral life can be sustained through the new dark ages which are already upon us. And if the tradition of the virtues was able to survive the horrors of the last dark ages, we are not entirely without grounds for hope. This time however the barbarians are not waiting beyond the frontiers; they have already been governing us for quite some time. And it is our lack of consciousness of this that constitutes part of our predicament. We are waiting not for a Godot, but for another —doubtless very different—St. Benedict.'[27]

Perhaps we don't need another Benedict. The old one will do very well.

---

27 Alasdair MacIntyre, *After Virtue* pp.244-5

10. Guests in a Monastic Culture

From time to time children come to visit our monastery. One boy wrote after such a visit, "We went up to the monastery door. We knocked on the door, and one of the monsters came out." One hopes that wasn't a reaction to Br Zachary's rather fierce appearance.

St Benedict makes it clear that we must welcome guests: 'All guests who present themselves are to be welcomed as Christ, for he himself will say: *I was a stranger and you welcomed me* (Matt 25:35).'[28] We don't have guests just because we ought to. We really do like having guests.

Guests are part of our life for, as St Benedict says, 'A monastery is never without them'[29]. They are a real enrichment of our life. Guests keep us in contact with the world around us. Many become our friends. Some come for spiritual direction, and we ourselves learn as much from them as they do from us. Their presence with us in church encourages us, augmenting this group of people worshipping God. Since we are in our monastery primarily to worship God, we are fulfilling our first call when we make it possible for other people to do the same.

It is a curious fact that as fewer and fewer people join monasteries, more and more want to visit us. There is a fascination with the life; people recognise that there is something important here for people trying to live Christian lives in a hostile world. Even some who are not Christian find in the rhythm and balance of life a welcome relief from the chaos and pressure of modern life. Many guests want to enter into some formal

---

[28] RB 53

[29] RB 53:16

relationship with the monastery, as tertiaries or oblates. Others are happy just to know that the monastery is there, some distance away, maybe, supporting them in their lives.

What guests seem to value most about the monastic life is the priority of God and the sense of rhythm. In today's society it is hard to maintain an awareness of the priority of God. God is constantly pushed to the edges as a kind of leisure time activity, an eccentric hobby for those who like that sort of thing. Even parish churches can struggle with this as they accept a vision of themselves as centres of community in a fragmented world. Their lives can be dominated by buildings, structures and various plans for outreach in a way which excludes God except as a kind of footnote. That a church should be a place of worship in which worship is offered every day, is a concept honoured far more in the breach than in the observance, even by churches that should know better.

By contrast, a monastery is for God. It is centred on God, directed to God and makes no sense at all without God. Yet that does not mean it is detached from the world. It is not an ivory tower separating its inhabitants from the world. Visitors to monasteries are often astonished at how well-informed nuns and monks are about what is going on in the world. Simply because of the space around them they seem able to see more clearly and understand more deeply the things that happen in society. A person who comes into a monastery in flight from the world will not make a good nun or monk. God cares passionately about the world and the people in it. He cares so much that he sent his Son to live and die for that world. So he wants his Christian sons and daughters to care about the world, pray for it and, when possible, directly help it.

The world outside the enclosure has gifts to give us who live within it. The monks and nuns themselves have come from this world: they are the world's first gift; their families and friends are an extension of that gift. Money, food, books, ideas and a host of other things come in from outside the enclosure and enrich our lives. We too have gifts to offer the world in a holy trafficking. Silence, space and a knowledge of God are some of them. Old values now lost can be rediscovered; new ways of arranging life and understanding the priorities of life can come from the cloister.

There is a healthy exchange between the cloister and the world. As Christians we are bound together in the same Body of Christ; the same blood goes through us all. Yet there needs to be a healthy distance between us as well. Funny clothes, walls and big grounds help to maintain this. We in the monasteries need to think constantly about how to use the internet, how many visitors to receive, how much work to accept, and when to say 'No'. If we fail to do that intelligently we lose the very qualities of our life that make us useful to the men and women living around us: we compromise the prayer that should be helping people thousands of miles away. Too much assimilation to the world saps the monastic life of its vigour and before long the monastery dies. That has happened countless times over the centuries.

Yet why do people like coming here? Often it is because we are counter-cultural. We do not automatically accept the priorities and values of the society around us. These values are not necessarily wrong but they don't fit our life. This makes it easier for our guests to examine these values of modern life for themselves and see whether they need correcting.

Spending a few days in a monastic community can give a good opportunity to sort out lives which have got complicated and stressful.

These values raise questions about the principles of life today which we examine in the next Chapter.

11. The Monastic Life as Counter-Cultural

a) Choice

Our world believes choice is a good thing. The more choice we have the happier we shall be. Supermarkets provide a vast range of different products to give us that choice. Politicians promise us choices of schools for our children, jobs for those who want them, doctors, hospitals and different kinds of treatment. People who come to church expect the service to meet their needs and move to a different church if it doesn't. Churches offer a wide range of different services so that people can choose which they prefer. Many people believe this freedom of choice should extend to friendships, sexual relationships and even children. People don't marry so they are free to change their sexual partners, to discard one and move on to another, or to enjoy several at once. Abortion, which some regard as the killing of an innocent child, is renamed 'a woman's right to choose.' People must be able to choose whether or not to have children, and whether they should be boys or girls. Some believe that they should be able to decide more and more about the genetic make up of their children.

Against this monks and nuns give up the right to choose. This is a major contradiction of the current belief that choice is essential to happiness. Yet people who have made this choice to give up choice are generally happy with it. How can we understand this?

First, of course, there are very few monastic communities today where all choice has disappeared. Small choices remain about the books you read, the time you get up or go to bed (within boundaries), how you spend a day off, even what you wear.

Secondly, even in bigger matters the choices are not usually imposed in a military fashion. There is discussion of needs and preferences. A wise superior considers a man or woman's abilities and tries to make sure they will flourish in whatever they are asked to do. Of course, there are many things we have to do which we may not like doing – washing up, cleaning, getting up early, but these things are necessary in any normal household.

And most importantly all this is based on the choice we have each made to live in this life. We give up complete freedom of choice by that choice freely made. We don't make the choice suddenly and without consideration. Generally there are several years in which we live the life before making that final choice for life. Marriages, of course, are intended to be for life and people go into them with that same awareness that choice becomes limited for the greater good of living out a relationship of love. Sadly many people leave their marriages. Sadly, too, many people leave religious life. But the ideal in both cases is to stay faithful to the end. Why should we stick it out even when it gets difficult?

We need to stay if we are going to grow. Plants do not like being transplanted. The bigger they are the harder it becomes. Oaks need time and stability to grow into the magnificent trees they can be. We too need to stay in relationships. All relationships have their difficult moments. Usually these difficulties come at the point of growth. Adolescents are difficult because they are growing physically and emotionally. They need space to grow, but they also need constraints that will help them to grow straight. All of us are basically selfish. Our first concern is ourself. When we marry, or make a friendship we have to consider someone else's needs as well as our own. If we don't do that the marriage will be abusive, or disastrous. If friends exist simply for our gratification they are not really friends; they are servants. Living together in a marriage is probably the most difficult part of any marriage; it is also the most worthwhile. The same is true in a religious community. That is why nuns and monks turn out to know a surprising amount about the challenges people have living in close relationships with others. The problem for us is that we don't really choose who we will live with. God sends us to a community. They may seem charming, delightful and open minded people, until we start living together; then the weaknesses appear. We find ourselves asking, can I really put up with his selfishness for the rest of my life? How can she seem to be so holy and yet insist on always having her own way? Does he know how annoying he is when he says that? If we are honest we also have to admit that we too are flawed. I may preach beautiful sermons, give very good counsel and write impressive books, and yet people can still find me difficult to live with.

This seems negative, but it needn't be. The best friendships are those which require some work. A good marriage needs times when husband and wife are forced really to think about what they are doing and how really to make it work. In community life we have a number of choices. We can simply avoid difficult people and live as far as possible apart from them; we can fight back with our own sins and selfishness; or we can follow the way of St Benedict and see that it is in the attention to all these difficulties of daily life that real growth happens: growth as human beings and growth in the spiritual life of learning to love the people whom God made and gave to live with us. We shall see more of that later in this book.

b) Celibacy

Of all the choices monks and nuns make the one that shocks people most is probably celibacy. Good faithful Christians are often as shocked about it as non-church people. Everyone assumes marriage is normal; or if not, that sex is normal and absolutely necessary for a healthy life. Those who don't have sex are assumed to be emotionally immature, repressed, maybe gay, or peculiar. Well, we can't claim that none of us who take a vow of celibacy is peculiar. There are peculiar people in religious communities as there are anywhere else in the world. Yet most of the men and women dressed in those funny clothes turn out to be perfectly sensible, emotionally well adjusted people. It really is possible to live a fulfilled healthy life without sex (in its narrow understanding of sexual intercourse). Human beings share a great deal with the animal kingdom; our drive to have sex in order to procreate is part of that. Unlike animals we are free to make a choice about that. When people assume that we must have sex they are actually downgrading us to mere animals which cannot choose. Curiously, by taking a vow of celibacy nuns and monks may not be devaluing sex, but actually giving it greater value. It is human to express love through sexual encounters. It is also human to find other ways of expressing love. We are not prisoners of our drive to procreate.

Curiously, too, St Benedict says nothing at all about celibacy. It is simply assumed to be part of our life. Do people today make too much of a big deal about sex? The sexual revolution of the Sixties has not really given people as much freedom as is supposed. It may even have made people more imprisoned by their animal desires. Actually, Philip Larkin was wrong to suggest (ironically) that sex began in 1963.[30] It has always been there in good and very bad forms. The difference now is that so many forms of sex have become acceptable which were once considered wicked. What is not clear is whether the new openness about sex has not really cheapened all that is good in it and made its destructive features more prevalent.

Why, then, do monks and nuns choose not to marry? Partly because it is simply a condition of the life. The word monk comes from the Greek word 'monachos' which simply means single. Monks have always been single and, because Christian morality has never allowed sex outside marriage monks and nuns have been expected to be celibate. Many, of course, have not lived up to that expectation. All of us know that our commitment to celibacy has been, to say the least imperfect. Clearly also different personalities have come to celibacy for different reasons.

For some the desire to serve God completely has made it clear to them that marriage was not possible. Others may have realised they are gay and, particularly before being gay was acceptable to society, have chosen to live in a community where at least there is a real human intimacy as well as the support to remain celibate.

There are bad reasons for being celibate: a fear of sex is one; a fear of close relationships or a selfish desire to remain alone is another. These fears or difficulties need to be left behind or resolved. A monk who is simply a confirmed bachelor is not responding to a call to give himself

---

30 'Sexual intercourse began
In nineteen sixty-three…' from *Annus Mirabilis* by Philip Larkin (1922-1985)

wholly to God. A person who cannot cope with close relationships will never be any good at community life.

Most people who have committed themselves to celibacy will find it hard at times. It is meant to be hard since sexuality is so close to our identity as human beings. If we choose to give it to God it leaves a gap, a space inside us, maybe even an aching wound. Our prayer is that God will fill this space with his love. If we let him, he will but that doesn't necessarily make it easier. His love will make us more loving, more compassionate, more vulnerable to others' needs. All love does this; married people discover this too. It is not always comfortable to live with vulnerability.

Love is creative. Love between a man and a woman, expressed sexually will produce children and will create an environment of love that makes it possible for those children to grow up as mature, well balanced men and women. Love in other contexts will have the same effect. How many children have found it was their grandparents or their aunts that gave them the love they needed when their parents were too busy or too distracted? How many unhappy or immature people have found new life in a close friendship or love affair? Love in a religious community will be expressed in different ways, according to the different personalities. It certainly does not involve a constant expression of hugs and enthusiastic affirmation. Yet the love is there and a new entrant will need to find it and give it if he or she is to find the creativity that will bring out all the best of their personality.

Love invites us to grow. Many who engage in sexual affairs do not grow in themselves. This is probably because they are simply taking their own pleasure, not giving themselves to the other. Love challenges us to move out of the safe, secure comfort zone we are used to and allow feelings we have not known, or an intensity we have never experienced to take us over. The inner self which may have kept itself safe for so long now bursts out of its cocoon and seems to be on fire.

Love is dangerous. Love between couples can turn to hatred and even to murder. A mother's love can become dangerously possessive and destructive. A father's love can be expressed in a demanding and intimidating expectation that the child always does well. Often we fend off love because we fear it will make demands on us. Or we refuse to give love because we don't want to get hurt.

C.S.Lewis writes movingly about this: 'To love at all is to be vulnerable. Love anything, and your heart will certainly be wrung and possibly broken. If you want to make sure of keeping it intact, you must give your heart to no one, not even to an animal. Wrap it carefully round with hobbies and little luxuries; avoid all entanglements; lock it up safe in the casket or coffin of your selfishness. But in that casket – safe, dark, motionless, airless – it will change. It will not be broken; it will become unbreakable, impenetrable, irredeemable. The alternative to tragedy, or at least to the risk of tragedy, is damnation. The only place outside heaven where you can be safe from all the dangers and perturbations of love is Hell.'[31]

Monastic life is not a place to hide from love or to keep safe the love that is buried in each one of us. Love can be given and received in ways that are not sexual and therefore do not break the commitment of celibacy. The different kinds of love we give to parents, children,

[31] C.S.Lewis, *The Four Loves*

friends and those in need should all be found in a monastery. It is the love that Jesus offered, and it led him to the Cross.

A personal example may help here. When I was in my twenties I found my brother, sister and most of my friends all seemed to be getting married. They wanted to settle down for life with one person. There was clearly a kind of nesting instinct turning them away from single life to one that was committed to a wife or husband. I felt none of this. I did not want to be tied down to one person. I liked children and enjoyed teaching teenagers but I didn't want my own. My need for commitment was fully taken up in mission life. I was passionate about teaching Latin to young people, about social justice, the struggle for racial equality and about God. I had no need for anything else. My friends and family may have wondered if I was immature, or gay, or unable to form close relationships, or uninterested in sex. They were too polite to ask this! None of these questions occurred to me. They still seem irrelevant. I could see an invitation from God drawing me into a life with him which promised the excitements of prayer amongst people I liked and work amongst the poor which I really looked forward to. Celibacy was part of an exciting package. How could I refuse it?

The point of this is that what probably looked like negative factors in my life, viewed from the standpoint of my generation in fact were extremely positive when seen as God's call. Looking back I would say that God prepared me for his call to celibacy by freeing me from the need to 'nest' as my contemporaries did.

Religious communities do not always handle celibacy well. It is not much talked about. It is seen as the necessary background to the life, rather than being itself a way of love. Monks and nuns need to talk together about how their celibacy can be loving and enriching, not just a sterile singleness. If talked about we speak of the convenience of not being married so we are free to respond to different calls of service. Or perhaps we stress that celibacy is just a necessary, sometimes painful part of the monastic package. In today's world, as religious brothers and sisters seek new ways of explaining their life to a world gone mad on sex, much more is needed. We need to show how celibacy itself is loving and creates relationships of intimacy which are not sexual but fruitful. We need to show how the inner self and the bodily self grow together and produce richer, more loving personalities. We need to show that the gap left in our deepest person by our gift of sexual intimacy to God, painful though it may be, has become a creative part of our life with God which leaves us with no regrets. If we don't do this we are simply not responding fully to God's love.

c) Lifestyle

There was a time when most people's lives were very well ordered. You worked five or six days a week from 9.00 till 5.00. You got a tea break and a lunch break. Of course, some people worked shifts covering really unsocial hours; others didn't work at all. They still lived quite regular lives.

Today it is different. Some people who have excellent jobs and salaries work 14 hours a day, six or seven days a week. Many people have flexible hours, and even flexible days working from home. Many people have no jobs, or only such occasional work as they can pick up in the gig economy. It is common now to work through lunch time especially if you are on a computer.

To many people this flexible pattern of work seems good, giving more freedom; yet it also has bad consequences. Meal times suffer. People need to eat sensibly and regularly for the sake of their health. It is common now for people not to bother about breakfast, especially if they are tired from working too late, or socialising too late. They skip lunch, or grab a sandwich. Dinner may be a take away or a frozen meal. The result of this lifestyle is too often burn out, break downs, stress and broken relationships.

By contrast, in a monastery life is governed by a timetable. Meals happen at the same time every day and you have to go. Before each meal is usually a service in church so the day is broken up. You cannot work too long. You have to stop and take a break and do something different. Days are long, beginning maybe before six a.m. and finishing around ten. But they are regular. This means monks and nuns seldom suffer from burn out, breakdowns or the other ills of modern life. The regularity of the life means that proper balance is achieved; a good rhythm is established. Visitors who come here to stay find themselves relaxing immediately into the space and the quiet. They go home determined to establish some kind of rhythm in their own lives and when they succeed life improves.

None of this is very complicated. It is easy enough to suggest patterns that will work in a person's life: stopping for meals is one of those. Not staying up late is another. Taking a proper day off is a third. It sounds a little boring, or old fashioned, or even like school. The fact is, it works. Many high powered London executives have found the simple attention to these routines have saved their health and their marriages and made it possible to enjoy their work again. It is simple, but not easy. It is important to realise that. Modern life is disordered, unbalanced and highly pressured if you have a job. It is probably still pressured if you don't have a job, but the pressures are different. If we want to establish a proper pattern and balance in the day that will help body and mind to flourish we have to work against the stream.That means standing out against what other people are doing. The culture of work, flexibility, instant communication and the tyranny of the mobile phone make it hard to establish a different way of life. In the monastery we accept the timetable because we want to. We came seeking this balance. We have found over the years that it has really worked well. If you want to do it in your own life you need to find the motivation: to take control of my work; to eat properly for the sake of my health; to avoid a heart attack, a stroke or the obesity that comes from unhealthy eating; to rediscover my family; to have time to do simple things like play with the kids, go for walks, or even go to church on a Sunday. All this seems rather clichéd, yet clichés exist because they are true.

Rules generally are thought to be a bad thing (though there is a passion now for putting laws through Parliament which are supposed to make our society function perfectly!) The message of monastic life is that simple rules make life better. It is not a good idea to embrace a complicated structure. Start with a few simple rules, even just one! Turn off TV and computers at 11.00. Have breakfast. Stop for half an hour's lunch. Put your phone somewhere where you can't check it every time it bleeps. Once those rules are in place and have become part of your life you will find your days have changed. People speak of the ancient monastic wisdom. It is not rocket science of the spiritual life. It starts with these simple little rules that anyone can do, if they try.

d) Mobile phones

A few years ago, I had to travel to a community of sisters on the eastern side of Germany. It was a simple journey: a Lufthansa flight from Manchester to Nuremburg via Frankfurt; at Nuremburg airport friends would meet me and take me to the sisters. We should be there by 7.00 pm. Then Lufthansa cancelled our flight from Frankfurt. They put me on a train which arrived in Nuremburg two hours later. Then I had to find another train to Hof, and from there an expensive taxi to Selbitz, arriving after midnight. Meantime my friends at Nuremburg had no idea where I was. They phoned the sisters who phoned my community. If only I had had a phone on me I could have saved us all so much trouble! I now never travel without a phone.

There is no doubt that mobile phones can be immensely useful, even life saving. They also become tyrannical. A phone call, or even a text takes absolute priority for many people. Conversations are interrupted, driving is made dangerous, meals are abandoned just because the phone has squeaked. Travelling on trains has become a misery for those who don't enjoy listening to other people's loud and boring conversations. It is extraordinary how wrapped up in themselves phone users can be with no idea of the impact their conversations are making on other people. What does St Benedict say about that?

Not surprisingly he says nothing, since phones and modern technology were more than a thousand years away. But he does establish some priorities and they can guide us in our use of phones.

i) God comes first. For those of us who try to live the Christian life, do we make sure that phones never get in the way of God?

Visitors to our monastery often leave their phones at home, or hand them in to us for safe keeping. They are delighted by the freedom this gives them. Do all of us make sure our phones are off when we are praying, reading, or keeping silence for God?

ii) Silence is essential to Benedict's life. Monks must be silent in the dormitory so they can sleep and wake up very early for the night office.[32] The oratory must be kept quiet so that brothers can pray.[33] Benedict lays out a careful timetable[34] and although he allows the timetable to be changed as local conditions demand he recognises as we do that timetables provide space for people to discover themselves and God. Noise of any kind invades that space and distracts us from dealing with ourselves. That is what phone conversations do, too.

iii) Brothers and sisters matter. Benedict spends a large part of the rule spelling out how to care for each other: the sick, the elderly, the young, the novices, those working, those travelling, those in authority and those who need to ask for things all get a special place in the Rule. Even those who have done wrong get several chapters describing how to put them right. Benedict tries also to keep the outside world at bay. Even bishops and other church authorities must not be allowed to interfere.[35] Does not this attention to the actual people around us suggest that those who phone us must be kept at an appropriate distance?

---

32 RB 22
33 RB 54
34 RB 8
35 RB 65: 3f.

iv) Words matter. They can be comforting, inspiring and informative; they can also be destructive. Phones and frequent use of social media encourage us to scatter words without thought. Politicians, who should know better, constantly get into trouble through careless emails and tweets. Benedict is so concerned about this that he urges his monks to refrain even from speaking good words.[36] Silence is better he says. In another chapter on Good Works he writes, 'Guard your lips from harmful and deceptive speech. Prefer moderation in speech and speak no foolish chatter.'[37] Benedict may sound a bit of a killjoy to us, until we try this for ourselves. We are drowning in words. Listen to news programmes and you realise how the same things are said over and over again, day after day. Newspapers churn out news with a sense of urgency and excitement that this may change the world. Read the same newspaper a couple of days later and you find most of it is irrelevant. Facebook, WhatsApp, Twitter and the other 'social media' seem to be giving us important information. In fact most of it is trivial. Far from deepening our understanding of the world, a very large part of the internet is trivialising it because it cannot distinguish between the really important pieces of information and the large amount of gossip.

v) Very often people come to our monasteries with major problems they think we can help them to solve. We are happy to talk with them. But we also leave them alone in the silence,

[36] RB 6:2
[37] RB 6:51f

the space or the worship in Church. Amazingly enough they sort out their own problems. Priorities reestablish themselves. God comes first. Family, values, or some other really important part of their life is seen in its proper place and the problems become manageable. This is why, in the end, we believe in silence, or at least a restraint in words. It really works!

e) Stuff!

"I have too much stuff!" This is a constant complaint from friends. Our modern world tells us that the more we have, the more we are. We need lots of money to buy lots of things; then people will admire us and see how important we are. People pursue this goal but do not find the happiness they seek. What has gone wrong?

A young woman recently visited Stanbrook Abbey with her mother. She was a fairly typical nineteen year old, with a couple of studs, and jeans torn at the knees. She went into the Abbey shop and came out with the Rule of St Benedict. Her mother wrote afterwards: "She stayed up that night to read the rule and came out in the morning declaring that she owned far too many things and needed to shed some possessions. It was much more important to live fully than to own things. She also said she needed to carry the Rule about with her, but hidden away so that no one would know."

It's not only secular people who have a problem with possessions. Monks have the same problem! I have always prided myself on how little I have. I genuinely don't want things. I buy clothes only when I really need them; I throw things away ruthlessly. So when I had to move my room in the monastery I thought it would be a work of a few minutes. In fact it took seven trips with a suitcase. I was appalled at how much I had gathered in a few years. How much more of a problem this is to people who live in houses, with all the expectations in modern life that clothes will be new and technology completely up to date! Yet, as we shall see in a later chapter our need for possessions is one of the host of factors which is destroying the surface of our planet, making it harder and harder to sustain human life. In Benedict's day they knew nothing of climate change or environmental degradation. Yet Benedict had a lot to say about possessions.

St Benedict is known for his kindness, gentleness and his moderation. Yet one of the few things he is really passionate about is that his monks should not have possessions. 'No one may presume to give, receive, or retain anything of his own, nothing at all.'[38] In saying this Benedict is reminding his monks to look to God for everything they need. He recognises, of course that brothers do need things and is emphatic that they should be given sufficient clothes, writing things, food and anything else they really need. But they must look to the Abbot, or the community of brothers to provide this. This is really important for life in community. Possessions build up a wall around us. They cut us off from others. This is true in a small monastic community. It is true also in society. Rich people cut themselves off from others. Poor people have to live close to each other because they can't afford big houses, but also because they need each other to survive. It is not only the rich whose lives are cluttered by possessions. Anyone who has had to move house discovers how much the average person collects these days. If we want

[38] RB 33:2

to change our lives, declutter them and get more meaning into them we need to start with the things we own.

Most people cannot live as monks or nuns. God does not intend this. We do need possessions – a place to live, clothes to wear, food to eat and all sorts of things necessary to daily life. Yet people constantly say, "I have too much stuff!" Can we set some priorities to get rid of stuff, or not collect it in the first place? Here are a few questions that may help:

1. Do I really need this? If not, can I get rid of it?
2. What is the effect of this stuff on the environment? We know the world is filling up with junk. We know that the world's resources are being used up creating things for us to buy. Can we at least cut back on our possessions as a way of saving the planet?
3. Does this stuff make me happy, or does it confuse my life? If stuff doesn't make us happy we need to look elsewhere for happiness.
4. Do my children really need piles and piles of toys? Everyone agrees that children need to be active, outside, not stuck in a roomful of toys, still less of computer games.
5. Jesus said it is hard for a rich man to enter the kingdom of heaven. We don't have to be very rich to realise that our possessions get in the way of our attention to God.[39]
6. We need to want to cut down on possessions because we want something better. If we simply do it out of guilt we will fail.

[39] Matthew 19:23

We need to find our own reasons for this – St Benedict wants his monks to focus on God and discover the real joy of life with Him. De-cluttering our life should help us to see God more clearly.

7. De-cluttering life should also help families to live together. Simple ways of entertaining children are better at creating relationships that parents can treasure, than giving them piles of toys to play with and discard.

8. The modern world tries to make us believe that we are what we possess so that we will buy more to become more. This is a lie. If we want to find out who we really are we need to get rid of the possessions that distract us. We will find we still exist, people still talk to us and we have more freedom to live. Curiously, the less we have, the more we are. One of the most loved of all saints was St Francis, yet he had nothing. If we can move in the direction of St Francis we will find there is much more to us than the things we own.

12. Valuing Our World

"I'm over 80. I don't produce anything. I'm of no value. I shouldn't still be around."

I heard this recently from a friend. It is, of course, not true, but many old people feel it is true and that says a lot about our society. They feel they have no value because our society values things and people according to the money they earn. However much people may talk of the value of beauty, old people, lovely countryside and all that make us human, money tends to trump them all.

Rich people are thought to be really important because they are rich. Top businessmen and industrialists deserve their million pound salaries because they make so much money for others to share in. Poor people are worth very little because they contribute very little. Unemployed people and refugees are a drain on the economy. They are a sort of aberration which shouldn't really exist, so we make the minimum possible allowance for them and hope they will go away.

I expect none of us thinks quite like that, but these do seem to be the values of our society and we easily go along with them. It certainly affects the way we think about the environment. We all know now that trees, grass, birds and insects matter. They matter in themselves because God created them. They matter also because they are essential for the health of the world we live in. But if we have a patch of ground doing nothing we think it is of no value until we sell it for 'development' (a euphemism for buildings that destroy grass, trees, insects and birds).

We know now that chemicals used to improve crops and destroy insects tend also to damage the soil. They may produce better crops in the short term, but in the long term they can be an environmental disaster. Yet farmers still use them. You make more money in the short term and money always trumps the long term destruction. That is true of the economy. Any argument in favour of preserving, or restoring our damaged world will be trumped by the argument for economic growth. Money is more important than anything. In America, in the election which produced Donald Trump as President many rich businessmen, who knew perfectly well what Donald Trump was like, still voted for him. Why? 'Because he is good for business.' The fact that Trump's policies might destroy the environment, raise global warming, alienate Muslims and Mexicans, and even start a war did not matter, compared with the short term making of money.

And all this is directly against the Gospel of Christ. Christ said it all in four words: "Blessed are you poor." (Luke 6:20) He was not being sentimental. He knew how hard life can be for the poor, but he knew they were much more likely to value God above all else, because they depend on God. The rich depend on their money for security so God comes a poor second (or third, or sixth!). The poor are also blessings to us. They enrich our lives, if we listen to them and let them share their knowledge of God with us. Again I am not being sentimental. That is how they are.

When Pope Francis was elected Pope a fellow cardinal told him, "Don't forget the poor", and he hasn't, so changing the face of Catholicism. It is the poor who suffer first because of the destruction of the environment. Their villages are destroyed by rising sea levels. Their livelihood as fishermen is destroyed by the plastic waste in the sea and the destruction of life in the ocean. Their farmlands become desert because of climate change. Yet it is they also who can teach the world how to live more simply so that the world is not destroyed. None of this is new. These are old truths which go back behind the Gospel to the time when the Jewish people were discovering the Law of Moses, or listening to the prophets Amos, Micah and Isaiah. They put the poor into the centre of God's message. The Law of Moses constantly puts care of 'the widow, the orphan and the stranger'[40] at the centre of the Law. The prophets castigate the rich for building big houses at the expense of the poor. If we ignore these great prophets and think the rich are more important, we are ignoring what God himself is saying.

What is new today is to see that the world we live in is like the poor. It is vulnerable. Trees can be chopped down; they can't defend themselves. Insects can be wiped out with chemicals; they can't fight back. Grass can be paved over. The fragile food chain which keeps us alive can be disrupted. If bees go, pollination goes and so do most of our crops. The sea is dying, poisoned by our rubbish. It is losing its oxygen; it cannot support the fish we like to eat. Nature and the seas can recover from the damage we have inflicted on it, but they need time and space. We do not give them time. Time is money. We spend all the time we have trying to make more money, then we spend the money destroying the world that supports us. In the end we believe if we can make enough money we can throw it at the problems of the environment and solve them. The very thing, the pursuit of money, which is destroying our world becomes the thing that is supposed to save it. Satan has won. The vicious circle devours everything while it pretends to be saving it.

---

[40] Exodus 22:21-24

Anyone who has worked among poor people knows how quickly you see them differently. People who looked dreary, drab, battered, even defeated are revealed as people with courage, resilience, generosity and a deep capacity for joy. We need to see the world of nature differently as well. A tree is not just a green thing at the end of a field. It is a home for birds; it is beautiful in its own right; it is an amazing machine taking poisonous gases out of the atmosphere and putting breathable gas back in. Boring looking grass does that too. Insects, looked at close, are delicate and complex. When we take time to look at the world around us we come to love it and cherish it, as we do the weaker and vulnerable people in our midst. Is it not part of our Christian heritage of care for the weak and vulnerable that we care for every part of it, not just out of self interest (we need the world of nature to stay alive) but because it is God's?

Monastic life cannot claim to be the only form of human life which actually cares for the environment. Care of the environment unites people across all kinds of religious, political and social divides. Yet we can claim that our form of the life, properly lived can make a real contribution to the struggle to change humanity's ways. Simplicity of life does discourage waste and encourage recycling. Monasteries with their large grounds are actually providing places where insects and birds can live, where bio-diversity can be preserved. Spending so much time in one place means that nuns and monks love the trees and plants that surround them and see them as gifts from God. Teaching people who visit us that life is more than work, possessions and endless entertainment actually cultivates an approach to life that counteracts destructive consumerism. Of course, we didn't invent this life, Jesus did that!

"Blessed are the poor. Blessed are the meek." Jesus wasn't talking in paradoxes. He was telling us what will save the world. Also, he is not telling us a Gospel that is actually bad news: that we have to be miserable, trapped in poverty and constantly down trodden to be 'blessed'. He is telling us that his way of being poor and meek actually sets us free and gives us a completely new understanding of life. "I came that they might have life, and might have it more abundantly."[41] Anyone who spends time living with the poor, especially in the so-called Third World, knows how exciting that can be. It is not always comfortable; roads are terrible, beds can be hard, sleeping conditions crowded, food boring; but it really brings one down to earth. You feel more real. You don't need all the things you think you need in the UK. And you have these marvellous people around you, people who are joyful, resilient and full of confidence that God is caring for them. It's a real privilege to be able to learn about God from them. Poor people are a real challenge to us in the religious life. They show us how much we fail to live the life to which we have been called. Pope Francis told us once to let the poor evangelise us.[42] Those of us living in monasteries need to take that much more seriously than we do.

---

[41] John 10:10
[42] Evangelii Gaudium 198

13. A Nun's Life

Interview with Sr Philippa

Q. What is the point of contemplative life in a monastery such as yours?

A. As I see it the Rule of St Benedict by which we live is entirely geared to living a life of love, that is allowing God's own life and love to flow through each of us to the whole world. An image occurred to me many years ago when I was still a novice – that each of us is like a burning glass helping to spread the fire of God's love over the world.

Q. Would you say you enjoy it?

A. Of course nobody can live at a high pitch of felt enjoyment all the time, but I most certainly can say that this life gives me a great deal of joy. Very often my heart is singing and I feel like a soaring bird.

Q. What do you most enjoy?

A. Mass is a high point of each day; feast days provide some wonderful texts and wonderful music, also very good food! And I greatly appreciate the opportunity of meeting so many people 'heart to heart.' They arrive as strangers for all kinds of reasons and a deep encounter makes us into friends even at the first meeting.

Q. Do you organise your prayer into different kinds of prayer such as adoration, thanksgiving, intercession?

A. No, I don't organise my prayer in this way. I often consciously try to allow myself to be drawn more deeply into the life of the Trinity (I take it that this is what Baptism effects in us) by praying 'Glory be to the Father and to the Son and to the Holy Spirit' – and often get no further than the Father. When I start to intercede for one person or situation I find that ripples go out wider and wider because I don't want to leave anybody out, but I usually drift away from intercession altogether and back to adoration. I do sometimes start out by consciously offering the whole suffering world to God, or by thinking of one particular great need, or by thanking God for one particular thing, but adoration usually predominates. When I have done or said something that I really regret I feel very acutely my need of God and that is one of the best ways of getting close to him.

Sometimes all I can do is BE THERE – or advert to the fact that God is present, and try to be present myself in at least some degree. Sometimes it is possible to savour the silence in such a way that it is quite enough. I find it helpful to listen with my physical ears as if I am straining to hear a distant melody – this is a good way of dealing with distracting thoughts.

Q. How do you give some focus to your prayer when distractions are crowding in?

A. I try to cope with distractions by looking at the Crucifix and trying to unite my tiny little emptying out of this distracting thought with the complete self-emptying of Christ. I find it much more difficult to pray outside our church with its huge absorbing Crucifix. It recently occurred to me that the widow who gave her all to the treasury in the Temple, unaware by whom she was observed, foreshadowed the complete self-emptying of Christ on the Cross to the extent that water came out with the last of his blood when the centurion opened his side with the spear. And each distracting thought is very small and insignificant but at the time can be my all.

Q. What part does Scripture play in your life?

A. We are exposed to a very great deal of Scripture every day, in the words of the psalms at each of the hours of the Divine Office, in most of the readings at both Mass and Office as well as in our private Lectio Divina. I am aware of the Word of God permeating my life, influencing the way I see people and situations, furnishing me with images and turns of phrase when I speak. Often the reading at meals from biographies, travel books or whatever seems to take up the same theme or idea as has been raised at Mass or in the Office. Life becomes ever more unified which is extremely satisfying.

Q. From the outside monastic life can look isolated and institutional. How could you describe it as a life following Christ as he appears in the Gospels?

A. I have often wondered why it was that the Desert Fathers and the monastic way of following Christ came before – and so many centuries before – the Franciscan life, which seems like a far more literal following of Christ as he appears in the Gospels. When I first heard the Lord calling me through the reading of the Gospel at Mass, in so far as I thought of what this would imply in a practical way, I think it was the 'active' kind of religious life that occurred to me. Two of my mother's sisters were active nuns. On reflection it seems to me that both historically and autobiographically it was the twin desires to 'be with as closely as possible' and to give everything in the most absolute way possible which made the monastic way of life so alluring.

Q. Can you give us some tips on how to do Lectio Divina?

A. I find it helps to use an unfamiliar translation of the Scriptures to wake me up to a passage which I have heard very often, perhaps without ever having really heard it at all. I have found Eugene Peterson's very free translation, or paraphrase, The Message, extremely helpful; and at the other extreme, I like looking up the Greek original of the New Testament. These two approaches can work together surprisingly well. It also helps to read the passage aloud, and it is excellent to do Lectio together with a friend who may have very different insights to one's own.

Q. Can you name any books you have found particularly helpful in your Christian life?

A. When I was reading English Literature at university I discovered *The Cloud of Unknowing* as literature – and later when I was a novice it became a firm favourite, as did *The Epistle of Privy Counsel* by the same anonymous author. One of my favourite bits is 'Take good gracious God as he is, plat and plain as a plaster and lay him to thy sick soul as it is….' Andre Louf's *Teach Us to Pray* was another book which fed me very deeply at that stage of my life. I copied out vast tracts of it, many of them extracts from Isaac the Syrian, but when I have tried in later life to read Isaac 'neat' as it were I have struggled. Simone Weil was never baptised but *Waiting on God* is one of the books that has influenced me most profoundly. It is her absolutism, holding nothing back which moves and inspires me. Albert Gelin's *The Poor of Yahweh* spoke to my heart in my early days. At the end of it in an appendix is a poem called *The Song of the Pariah, the Barber* which thrills me. The poor man knows he has nothing whatever to offer the Lord, the Spirit of Blessing, and is thrilled to be allowed to follow him, simply to be near him.

Q. St Benedict wrote his Rule for men and women in community. Why is it important for us to live the life in community?

A. St Basil said that if one lives alone, whose feet would one wash? Community provides many opportunities for serving the Lord in the person of one's brothers or sisters, and also of being served by them. We have such different gifts of mind and heart as well as training and experience so we can be of great help to one another. We can also offer the gift of gracious acceptance of the help of others. It is important that we each accept both our gifts and our limitations, using both for the good of the whole.

Q. How do you deal with conflicts in community?

A. I don't think we are good at dealing with conflicts in our community. It is one of the areas we can see the need for growth under the inspiration of the Holy Spirit. In theory I believe that one of the keys to thorny issues and differences of opinion is to speak directly to the person concerned rather than to complain behind their back. This way also has the benefit of being a great deal more likely to effect the desired change! Obviously it is also important to be willing to listen to the frank speaking of others! I think it is very important that we try to avoid the blame culture so prevalent at present in the world. It seems to me that each of us, no matter how small or insignificant, has enormous responsibility and enormous power, to speak the truth in love. I remember as a novice hearing one of my fellow-novices say “we don’t count”. I believe everybody counts and it is false humility to deny that I do.

Q. Why do you think you find conflict difficult? Is this something we share with most families and groups in our society?

A. The words that immediately occur to me are cowardice and laziness. It is more trouble to face conflicts. It shows much more respect of other people to be prepared to disagree and discuss with them. It is more truly loving than pretending to agree or just taking the line of least resistance. There are many people who have the need to be always right, always to have the last word; I know I avoid talking with them if I can – and that this is not a creative way of behaving.

Q. Do you miss not being able to go out when and where you please?

A. No, I can’t say I do.

Q. Why not?

A. There always seem to be so many interesting things to do and interesting people to see right here at Stanbrook. There was a time when I did quite a lot of travelling – to various monastic meetings round this country as well as trips to South Africa when first my father and then my mother were ill and could no longer come to England. There are places I would love to visit or to re-visit but I am very much aware of the tremendous hassle involved and am quite content to remain here, especially as we are now allowed to walk in the forest. I don’t recall ever feeling restricted by the enclosure.

Q. In our discussions for this book we have talked very little about the differences between Anglican and Roman Catholic churches. Does that surprise you?

A. No, I think I always tend to look for grounds of agreement rather than difference, no matter who I am with, and in the case of our book the points of convergence – living by the same Rule, and our common African heritage, represent very strong bonds of unity.

Q. Having said that, what do you value about being a Roman Catholic?

A. The answer that occurs to me is 'the poetry of the Catholic Church', its amazing richness of symbolism, its art, music, its long long tradition, its profound unity, the way the huge web is held together in unity. And I believe it is true.

Q. How can we contribute to the unity of the Church?

A. I think we can all contribute greatly to the unity of the Church by treating all others with respect, really listening to them. This applies also to people completely outside the boundaries of the Church – we can contribute to the unity of the whole family of humankind by respectful attention, giving our time, our concern and our prayers. I believe firmly that each of us has great responsibility and great power, great influence.

Q. I see Stanbrook has a couple of young sisters joining. What brings a young woman today into this kind of life?

A. I don't know but I imagine that they feel called to spend their 'one wild precious life'[43] in a way that will change the world. I think

---

[43] Mary Oliver. 'The Summer Day'

again of the generosity of the widow with her mite. Nobody can give more than their all.

Q. Do you take any interest in politics?

A. My interest in politics is very selective. I tend to turn off when it comes to internal divisions in the UK especially since what I regard as the total disaster of the Brexit vote, but I am vitally interested in the politics of Zimbabwe and South Africa.

Q. What issues really bother you about today's political world?

A. I am very concerned about climate change. And about the huge injustices that go on all around us. Innocent people in prison. The enormous injustices perpetrated by the welfare state.

Q. You have spoken in your biography of your life as an adventure. How is it that?

A. I have a stronger and stronger sense of the utter wonder of my life, the feeling that I am part of a network of relationships, that every detail of my life is held safely in God's hands, that he can bring good out of everything. I have an increasing desire to pour out my whole self like a libation.

Q. If death is an adventure how can we prepare for it?

A. By living to the full! By taking risks, growing in courage, enlarging our comfort-zones.

Q. What would you like to achieve before you die?

A. I'd like to give away as much as possible of myself, and also clear away as much as possible of the huge amount of clutter that has accumulated in my cell and the library office. I remember the saying of St John of the Cross that if a bird is held down by a silken thread it is as unfree as if it is chained. I'm a long way from the silken thread…

14. And Finally

Why do people join monasteries? In the end it is because of God. St Benedict writes: 'Seeking his workman in a multitude of people the Lord calls out to him and lifts his voice: "Is there anyone here who yearns for life and desires to see good days?"'[44] God calls us to this life. Without him it makes no sense. It is not a lifestyle choice. There may be many things in the life that attract us: the opportunity to study, the music in church, the particular works each community may do, teaching, pastoral care, spiritual direction or even working in the garden. These are good and necessary and they give clothing and shape to the call of monastic life. But it is God who calls. And we need to respond from the heart. If that happens 'We shall run on the path of God's commandments, our hearts overflowing with the unspeakable delight of love.'[45]

Of course it is not quite as simple as that! There is a lovely story in Lewis Carroll's *Through the Looking-Glass and What Alice Found There* telling how Alice came out of a cottage and saw a hill in front of her. She started to walk towards it and found herself going back into the house. Three times this happened. In the end the Rose told her to walk in the opposite direction. She did this and found herself walking towards the hill. Christian life often goes in the opposite direction from what we expect.

Most of us joining the religious life probably imagine that our lives will move steadily forward in a nice ordered fashion. We think we will

---

[44] RB Prologue 14
[45] RB Prologue 49

acquire more and more knowledge, we will get better and better at praying, and we may even end up quite holy. Sadly it doesn't seem to work out like that at all. After many years of religious life we can feel we have learned nothing at all. There is a story of a saintly old monk on his death bed muttering "But, Lord, I haven't started yet." That, maybe, is what the life is really about, and it applies to all Christian life.

St Antony of Egypt once said, "If you think you are praying, then you are not." In prayer we can't be thinking about ourselves or worrying about how well we are performing. We have to be thinking of God. In the same way, we can't be self consciously good, or holy. Christians often worry about whether they are growing in the spiritual life, why their prayer does not seem to get better or why they don't feel they are overcoming their sins. It's not our job to worry about that. If we do, we tend to become self focussed. The devil makes us anxious. He distracts our attention from God and gets us to worry about ourselves. Truly holy people do not worry about themselves. They know they are small, weak, often ignorant, and still sinners, but it doesn't matter since God is wonderful and God loves us whether we are good or not.

Jesus died on the Cross so that we might be set free from sin and be able to enter the presence of God. There is nothing we can do to earn the right to enter the presence of God. Jesus has bought us that privilege. We just need to receive it. Receiving it will have consequences. We try to respond to what Christ has done by living our lives in the way he would like. What matters, though, at the end of life is that we should know that God accepts us freely because he loves us, not because we have built up an impressive stock of goodness, or because we have become particularly fine people. The stories of the Prodigal Son[46], the Tax Collector[47] and the Woman who washed Jesus' feet[48] tell us that. Monks and nuns are not super-Christians. If there is a way of measuring holiness we know it is found just as often outside the monastery and amongst surprising people as it is within.

All we can claim is that we have tried to follow Christ; we have tried to serve God on the road to which he called us. If we can finish that journey with joy and thanksgiving for all that has passed then it has been worth it. Isn't that true of all of us human beings as we come to the end?

Yet again there is more. St Augustine catches it in his Confessions: "Late have I loved you, beauty so old and so new: late have I loved you. … You called and cried out loud and shattered my deafness. You were radiant and resplendent, you put to flight my blindness. You were fragrant, and I drew in my breath and now pant after you. I tasted you, and I feel but hunger and thirst for you. You touched me, and I am set on fire to attain the peace which is yours."[49]

In the end that is why we live this monastic life.

---

[46] Luke 15:11ff
[47] Luke 18:9ff
[48] Luke 7:36ff
[49] Confessions of Saint Augustine 10:27 translated by Henry Chadwick